Liberating Youth
from Adolescence

Liberating Youth
from Adolescence

Jeremy Paul Myers

Fortress Press
Minneapolis

LIBERATING YOUTH FROM ADOLESCENCE

Cover image: Thinkstock 2018 Kid's shadow on zebra crossing by AlexLinch
Cover design: Alisha Lofgren
Typesetting: PerfecType, Nashville, TN

Print ISBN: 978-1-5064-3343-1
eBook ISBN: 978-1-5064-3818-4

In memory of you, Dad.

You loved me and you made me laugh.
Every single day.

CONTENTS

INTRODUCTION

The caged bird sings
with a fearful trill
of things unknown
but longed for still
and his tune is heard
on the distant hill
for the caged bird
sings of freedom.[1]

I often say I love kids more than I love Jesus. I think Jesus is okay with this sentiment. In fact, I think Jesus prefers it this way. He can handle it. Jesus knows our young people are caged birds like the ones in Maya Angelou's poem. I write this book to change the way we think about our young people so that we might love them as they are, not as we think they should be. In some sense, this is a book about theology and ministry; but it is only a book about theology and ministry because it is a book about young people. If you have come looking for a new program or a silver bullet, then you have come to the wrong place. If you have come to have your eyes, ears, and heart opened to young people in new ways, then read on so you might learn to recognize this song of the caged birds.

Who Is This Book About?

Our practices of youth work grow out of our views of children and youth. I say *youth work* rather than *youth ministry* because I am including more than the church in this statement. Our views of children and youth influence the way we educate young people, the way we coach them, the way we raise them, the way we interact with them in the neighborhood, and the way we engage them in ministry. So, if we want our practices with young people to change and improve, then we must first examine our understanding of who they are. This book will help you do just that. It will change the way you understand who our young people are.

I intentionally use the term *young people* throughout this book for several reasons. First, it is meant to be inclusive of those we often consider children as well as those we call adolescents or young adults. We should not ignore the unique changes that occur during childhood and adolescence. However, too often we become fixated on these changes as the factors that define a person in these life phases rather than allowing the individual, as a child of God, to be the defining factor. The intention is not to wipe away the differences of people at these ages but to intentionally move us away from the silos created by developmental stage theories, which I will critique in this book. I avoid the terms *adolescent* and *adolescence* except when referring to them as words used by certain theories to describe this age group. I also use the term *adolescent* as a descriptor for the caricature our society has of the typical teenager, "the adolescent." *Adolescent* and *adolescence* come from the Latin word *adolescere*, which means *to ripen*. These words force us to understand this part of life as primarily about growth or ripening or becoming—as life yet to be achieved. This is a destructive way to think about our young people, so I refrain from using these words in this text. This book is not about children or kids or adolescents. It is about young people.

What Will Happen in This Book?

Walter Brueggemann claims we all live our lives in bondage to the dominant script. This is the script of "therapeutic, technological, consumerist militarism."[2] It leads us to believe we should always be happy and comfortable (therapeutic), we can solve any problem (technological), we have the right to own and consume whatever we want (consumerist), and we have the right to use force to protect this "American Dream" (militarism). This dominant script promises to make us safer and happier, but it has not. It has failed us, and we are less happy and more afraid than ever before. The dominant script rarely, if ever, liberates. It most often enslaves. This book challenges the current dominant script of adolescence, which is threatening the well-being of our young people. I will replace it with a theologically constructed counter-script of vocation and liberation for our young people.

As you will see in chapter 1, adolescence as we know it emerged during the same time Brueggemann's dominant script was taking root in the United States. The two, adolescence and this dominant script, are insepa-

> This book challenges the current dominant script of adolescence, which is threatening the well-being of our young people.

rable. The same worldview that gave rise to this therapeutic, techno-logical, consumerist militarism also gave rise to the primary narratives that shape the way we think about young people: developmental-stage theories and materialism. Both have had devastating effects on our understanding of young people and, therefore, also on our practices of ministry with young people.

This book weaves two disciplines, positive youth develop-ment and critical youth studies, together to (1) illuminate how our understanding of young people is rooted in both stage theo-ries and materialism, and (2) begin constructing a counterscript, a story of our liberation from bondage to this dominate narra-tive. The discipline of positive youth development has become an important corrective in response to traditional developmental-stage theories. Richard Lerner tells us "we simply can't argue for the existence of a 'typical' teenager or believe that any single conception [or stereotype] of adolescence is generally true. . . . Development isn't simple but incredibly multifaceted."[3] The field of critical youth studies has also offered an important corrective to the materialistic ways of understanding our young people by lifting up the ideals of youth voice and agency. Critical youth studies refuses to see young people as passive recipients of oppressive culture but rather sees them as empowered agents of change. The third, and most potent, strand woven into this counterscript is the theological concept of vocation, or God's call to serve our neighbor in freedom. This book offers you a vocational theory and theology of young people.

The dominant script gives rise to a particular stereotype of young people—which I will call the *undeveloped consumer*. The vocational theory of young people offered in this book helps us construct the counterscript, or antidote, to the undeveloped consumer. I will refer to this antidote as the *called cocreator*. Each of these, the undeveloped consumer and the called cocreator, seeks to answer young peoples' most pressing questions, but they do so in very different ways (see figure 1). Our assumptions and stereotypes of our young people perpetuate this myth of the undeveloped consumer, telling our young people they are undeveloped, identity-less, self-centered consumers. Our current practices of ministry are also unknowingly dependent

> The same worldview that gave rise to this therapeutic, technological, consumerist militarism also gave rise to the primary narratives that shape the way we think about young people.

upon this myth. Therefore, this project seeks to liberate our young people and ourselves from this myth. The called cocreator is not *undeveloped* but *called by God*; not *identity-less* but a *child of God*; not *self-centered* but *relational*; not a *consumer* but a *cocreator*. Our young people are singing like caged birds. Our young people find themselves trapped in the cage of the undeveloped consumer, but they are singing because, deep in their bones, they know another way to live. They are singing of the freedom that comes from God. The called cocreator embodies this freedom.

Who Is This Book For?

If you have read this far, then this book is for you. It is for those who care deeply about young people and how we engage in ministry with young people. It is for those who recognize something is deeply wrong with our practices of youth work and youth ministry that we cannot easily fix, but who hold some hope that many things are also deeply right. This book is practical enough that people will find it immediately helpful in their ministry with young people. It is also provocative enough to create meaningful discussion in the classroom at the undergraduate or seminary level. It is for lay leaders, volunteers, pastors, and students of ministry. It will work best if read and discussed with other partners in ministry. Long story short, it is for you.

Pressing Question	Undeveloped Consumer	Called Cocreator
What can I contribute to the world?	You are *undeveloped*. You are unable to fully contribute until you have arrived at adulthood.	You are *called* by God to use your gifts and abilities to serve God's world right now.
Who am I?	You are *identity-less*. You must seek or construct your true identity before you can become a competent adult.	God names you and claims you as a *child of God*. This is not an achievement but a gift.
Am I connected to anyone?	You are *self-centered*, so it does not matter. You are only concerned for your own well-being and happiness, which makes it difficult for you to connect with anyone.	You are a *relational* being. God has created you for relationships. There is no other way to think of yourself than connected to everything around you.
What is the purpose of my life?	You are a *commodified consumer*. You can help society by doing your part as both a commodity that is consumed by capitalism and as a consumer who consumes other commodities to keep capitalism running smoothly.	You are a *created cocreator*. God has gifted you and called you into the holy work of cocreating God's kingdom with God. You have power and attributes that cannot be commodified or consumed.

Figure 1: The Undeveloped Consumer vs. the Called Cocreator

How Is This Book Different?

I had the privilege of studying with Dr. Andrew Root while completing my PhD at Luther Seminary in Minnesota. One of the most provocative things I have heard Root talk about in recent years is his description of youth ministry as a technology. He says, "Technology is science used for functional ends, to achieve or solve some problem that will result in increased capital. This capital could be economic, social, or cultural [even religious]."[4] He goes on to critique popular practices of youth ministry as technology. We implement certain practices with the hope they will solve "some problems" for us. Most books about ministry today only offer another technology we hope will solve our problem, no matter how we define that problem. Instead, Root encourages us to leave the technological behind in favor of the theological. This book offers hope rather than technology. It is theological in that it seeks to construct a theological understanding of our young people. It is hopeful in that it takes root in God's promises and presence. You will not find a new technology in this book, but you will find an old hope.

This book is also different because it is not simply diagnosing a problem or describing a current situation but is seeking to proclaim hope and good news into that situation. The narratives of adolescent development and emerging adulthood, which are narratives we love kicking around in ministry, are helpful in that they describe what is going on. However, they fall short in that they do not help us see "the way things really are" or "what really is." Theologian Philip Hefner uses these phrases to describe what it means to think theologically about our lived realities.[5] So, developmental-stage theory might help us understand how young people experience change in their lives today, but it does not help us understand who young people are in light of God's promises. This book offers a hope-filled theological construction of the way things really are for our young people as God's children.

Who Is the Author?

Today, authors cannot and should not offer their opinions without also disclosing their social locations. My perspective grows from my life experiences in particular contexts. These experiences both illuminate and limit my perspective. I write as one who has known privilege and power in his life. I am a white, Christian, straight, cisgender male who grew up Lutheran in the American Midwest. I spent my childhood in the lower-middle class, but I now find myself as an adult in the upper-middle class. I have known hard times, but I have never known oppression. I understand many opportunities have come my way, including authoring this book, floating down this river of privilege I inhabit.

> This book offers a hope-filled theological construction of the way things really are for our young people as God's children.

However, I also write as one committed to sharing my power and acknowledging how privilege grossly limits my imagination. Family members, friends, colleagues, mentors, and students have pushed back against my privilege and helped me see my place in our shared world in new ways. Therefore, I write as one who offers his voice to the long conversation, hoping that others will join it to affirm, challenge, deconstruct, and build upon what this project offers. Monologues do not usher in the kingdom of God, but dialogues might. I hope this book helps us all see where the holes are in our vision of young people so more people with other perspectives might come along and offer their wisdom into this conversation as well.

1

The Undeveloped Consumer: Youth in Bondage to the Adolescent

If I ask you to list the stereotypes adults have of teens, you would probably have no problem completing the task. What are some of the adjectives you would use? *Lazy, selfish, hyper, addicted to technology, inappropriate, smelly, horny, insecure, overconfident, loud, inconsiderate?* But if I ask you to create a list of stereotypes that apply to teenagers *only*, there is no way you can complete the task. Think about it for a moment. We often say teens are absent-minded. (1) Is absent-mindedness reserved for the teenage years? No. (2) Are adults ever absent-minded? Yes. (3) Have you experienced a young person not being absent-minded? Yes.

You can repeat these three questions for every stereotype used to describe teens, and you will end up with the same three answers. Try it. Insert your own stereotypes in the blanks below and see if the answers match your own.

1. Is _____ reserved for the teenage years? *No.*
2. Are adults ever _____? *Yes.*
3. Have you experienced a young person not being _____? *Yes.*

If these adjectives describe people in all age categories, and if their opposites are often true of teens, then why do we allow these characteristics to define and dominate the teenage years? We have come to believe in a caricature of our young people, which I will refer to as both *the adolescent* and *the undeveloped consumer*. Such a misunderstanding causes damage to our young people, limits them with low expectations, and holds them in bondage. Although the life-stage of *adolescence* might be a real thing with its own set of unique biological and social changes, "the adolescent" is a myth. We feed this myth when we assume those in this stage of life are primarily defined by the changes they experience rather than allowing them to define who they are as children of God with indispensable gifts for God's world.

We inadvertently created this caricature of the adolescent in the early 1900s through the convergence of unproven scientific theories, social shifts, and economic fluctuations.[1] The adolescent, which has become very convenient to adult society, is humorous, hyperbolic, and provides endless plot lines for PG-13 movies. However, at its worst, it is dangerous and threatens to dehumanize our young people.

Our dependence upon this myth of the adolescent has become a haunting, hidden, and powerful source of bad news in the lives of our young people. Theologian Douglas John Hall describes ministry as the church's work to discern the good news that will displace someone's bad news. This bad news is always the result of our collective and individual sin and brokenness. But the bad news will always sound and look different from one time and place to another. The good news will also be Jesus, but Jesus will always sound and look different from one time and place to the next. To proclaim Christ is to proclaim that which liberates an individual or community from sin's bondage. If this bondage is alcoholism, then the good news is sobriety. If this bondage is hate, then the good news is reconciliation. If this bondage is the myth of the adolescent or undeveloped consumer, then we will find liberation in the proclamation of the created cocreator. The bad news is always sin, but it manifests itself in a variety of ways. The good news is always Jesus, who will always manifest in the good news that displaces this bad news.[2]

The bad news becomes worse when we factor in the reality of intersectionality for so many young people who are minoritized, queer, undocumented, living in poverty, experiencing homelessness, and so on.[3] If we wish to proclaim good news to our young people, then we must do the hard work of hearing and understanding this particular source of bad news. An understanding of the historical emergence of the adolescent and its influence on youth ministry reveals two things. First, its characteristics are social constructs rather than biological inevitabilities. Second, it has become a powerful force of oppression and bondage in the lives of our young people. Intersectionality amplifies this oppression. Recognition of this caricature's origins also helps us deconstruct this collective cultural myth so our ministries might liberate young people, rather than retaining them in the bondage of a caricature.

The Historical Emergence of the Adolescent

The adolescent as we know him—a young person who is no longer a child but not yet an adult, who seems to struggle to find meaning and purpose in life—is only about one hundred years old. Prior to the twentieth century, you were either a child or an adult. If your body was able to contribute to the well-being of society through some form of work (i.e., homesteading, homemaking, farming, mining, hunting, millwork, etc.), then you were a contributing adult. Adults saw those in their teen years as smaller adults who had some growing and learning to do but were nonetheless ready and able to contribute. With the dawn of the twentieth century came new concerns and new ideas. The adolescent emerged from certain cultural phenomena of this time. These phenomena include (1) the idea of a necessary moratorium for young people, (2) a set of three social anxieties, (3) the Great Depression, and (4) the rise of compulsory public high school as the normal experience for teenagers. These phenomena molded Western society's image of young people. The mold, in turn, has become a self-fulfilling prophecy as it has mass-produced this caricature of the adolescent.

Moratorium

The first cultural phenomenon to influence our view of young people was the unfounded theory that young people need a moratorium to become healthy adults. Many consider American psychologist G. Stanley Hall to be the first child psychologist. He was concerned about young people arriving at adulthood with every ounce of their vigor and creativity. The term he adopted to describe adolescence was "storm and stress," a term that originated in German literature—not science.

Hall's image of the storm and stress of teenage years was a rushing mountain stream. The stream's purpose was to reach the lake below intact. We cause irreparable harm to the stream, the mountainside, and the lake below when we attempt to dam up the stream or divert its course. According to Hall, the same was true for adolescence. He was certain the trials and tribulations of adulthood, when introduced too early in one's life, zap the youthful vigor and creativity right out of the young person. Hall's solution was to prescribe a moratorium. A moratorium is a period defined by lack of serious responsibility, of self-reflection, and of recreation. Such a moratorium is necessary for the natural storm and stress of adolescence to run its course so the young person arrives at adulthood with their full capacity. Even though Hall's theory was not based on any empirical evidence and has since been debunked, it was still incredibly influential in the early twentieth century, and its influence still lingers today.

Societal Anxieties

The concept of storm and stress and its necessary moratorium gained traction in the context of some pervasive social anxieties of Americans in the early 1900s. Nancy Lesko identifies three sets of worries that occupied the thoughts, lifestyles, and policies of twentieth-century Americans, whether they were aware of them or not.[4] First, we were worried about race relationships. What would be the proper relationship between the various racial identities coexisting together in America? Second, we were worried about gender roles. Industrialization, urbanization, and the world wars all pushed against "traditional" gender roles. What role should a person play in this new society? Third, we worried about nation building. What would it mean for America to be a—or *the*—global superpower? These three issues were the sources of great anxiety across American society, and they impacted the way we raised our kids at the time.

The country was in a time of upheaval in all three of these areas. Jim Crow laws were the norm in the American South. There was tension between those who saw racism as the problem and those who saw integration as the problem. The roles of women were also changing as many began working and remaining single later into life. The flapper of the Roaring Twenties became a symbol of the new American woman. Would society survive if the pillars of traditional gender roles became unstable? The entire world was becoming more connected and less stable as well. We were entering a time of world wars and the deadliest century of human history. America was an emerging world power but was still developing its fledgling infrastructure and still healing from its own civil war.

Lesko sees Hall's unfounded theory of storm and stress and moratorium as extremely convenient for a country trying to solve its anxieties through its young people. She illuminates how adolescence became a technology of sorts, designed to transform something not useful (the child) into something useful (the adult).[5] The technology of adolescence is where America channeled its anxiety around race relations, gender roles, and nation building. We became obsessed with ensuring young people emerged from the moratorium of adolescence with a clear (and rigid) understanding of what it meant to be appropriately raced, gendered, and patriotic. We had convinced ourselves that a young person must simultaneously be free enough to discover himself while also systematically telling him who he had to be.

> We had convinced ourselves that a young person must simultaneously be free enough to discover himself while also systematically telling him who he had to be.

The Great Depression

The third cultural phenomenon to converge with the idea of moratorium and the societal anxieties of the time was the Great Depression and subsequent child labor laws. The National

Child Labor Committee (NCLC) formed in 1904, the same year Hall published his book, *Adolescence*. The NCLC's goal was to remove children from the work force. This goal was honorable and necessary. Many children were injured or killed due to unsafe conditions in the workplace. Fighting for their well-being was the ethical thing to do. The NCLC had children's best interests in mind, and Hall's theory of moratorium was exactly what they needed to make their case. However, they struggled to pass legislation that would protect children and remove them from the workforce.

In 1929 the stock market crashed, which led to massive job layoffs and the Great Depression. We removed child laborers from what little workforce there was to free up jobs for unemployed adults. The NCLC experienced a newfound acceptance of their agenda, and in 1938 Congress passed the Fair Labor Standards Act, making nearly all forms of child labor illegal.

There are a few important things to note about this phenomenon. First, it is significant and telling that we were not able to pass the Fair Labor Standards Act when its sole motivation was the well-being of our children. The act passed only when adult jobs and the nation's economy were at risk. History shows we are far more willing to mobilize for the sake of the economy than for the sake of our young people. Second, up until this point young people had always worked side by side with adults throughout the day. Although the removal of young people from the workforce was the ethical thing to do, it was also the beginning of what is now the very normal segregation of young people from adults. Adolescence was slowly becoming a very different time of life than childhood and adulthood, and the adolescent was becoming an enigma under a microscope.

High School

The fourth cultural phenomenon to shape our image of the adolescent, and widen the growing chasm between youth and adults, was the normalization of the American high school. Up until this point, only privileged families were able to access education for their children. They were not dependent on their children's income, and they either lived close to a school or could afford a boarding school. Rural families and families who depended on their teens' wages were rarely able to send their children to school. Schools were primarily places that reinforced religion, high culture, and manners. Students attended school to become civilized. Their reasons for attending school changed with post-Depression technological advances. The nature of work changed and began requiring skilled labor such as accounting, computing, and typing. Skilled labor required professional or technical training. Schools took on this role and shifted from reinforcing civilized high culture to teaching students how to type, compute, and calculate. These changes were both a response to the changing nature of work as well as the societal anxiety around nation building. If America was going to be a world power, we needed a well-educated and well-trained workforce.

By the early twentieth century, elementary school was mandatory for younger children. But it was not until the 1930s and

1940s that we began requiring teens to enroll in high school. In 1930, less than one-half of American teenagers were attending high school. By 1940, more than two-thirds of American teenagers were attending high school. We mandated young people to be around one another all day every day and to interact less and less with adults. This, in turn, intensified the impact of the peer relationship while weakening the impact of adult relationships.

These four phenomena converged over the first half of the twentieth century to create the petri dish in which youth culture and the adolescent grew. Hall's moratorium bracketed the teen years as a unique time of life when important changes must happen. His theory gained traction due to the societal anxieties or worries of the time around race relations, gender roles, and nation building. Moratorium became thought of as a universal technology, much like the conveyor belts and factories of the time, to produce the ideal product: if we universalize the adolescent experience, then we can guarantee the successful mass production of the kinds of adults we think we need. The removal of young people from the work force left them with nothing to do and nowhere to do it. Mandatory high school became the perfect place to enact the technology of adolescent moratorium for droves of unoccupied young people. Compulsory high school created a hothouse where youth culture began to grow. World War II sent large numbers of men and women off to war, creating opportunities for part-time jobs for high-school students. Extra income from these part-time jobs and the growing chasm between adult society and youth society fueled the growth of youth culture so that by the late 1940s and early 1950s you have, for the first time in history, a youth culture that is distinct from adult culture. Young people dressed and danced differently than adults; they listened to different music, talked differently, and socialized differently. The caricature of the American adolescent had been born. And we did not even know what we had done.

The Undeveloped Consumer

I hope you are beginning to understand the origins of the stereotypes you listed earlier in this chapter (p. 11). We bought into the pseudoscience of early adolescent developmental psychology. We adopted its theories because they were in full support of our superstitions and anxieties. We leveraged these theories to enact policies that have shaped generations of teenagers. Yet we still believe the adolescent, as a caricature, is a universal and inevitable phenomenon. These misconceptions still profoundly shape our perceptions of adolescents. From this point on, I will refer to this caricature as the *undeveloped consumer*. This undeveloped consumer is not who our young people truly are, nor is it who we want them to be. It is, however, what we have collectively come to expect from them. The adolescent as undeveloped consumer has four primary characteristics, all mistaken

> This undeveloped consumer is not who our young people truly are, nor is it who we want them to be.

assumptions made by adult society—we assume they are *undeveloped, identity-less, self-centered, commodified consumers.*

Undeveloped

It is not uncommon to hear adults explain the behavior of young people as typical behavior for the undeveloped—boys will be boys, kids will be kids. To be undeveloped is to be not quite fully human. At least this is the message we send when we talk about young people—their bodies, their relationships, their brains—as not yet fully developed. While it is true we develop over the course of life, we do so in fits and starts. In fact, development is often one step forward and two steps back. Development (or the movement toward older ages) is not linear, nor is it predictable or progressive.

To say a young person's brain is undeveloped—or his emotions, or her body, or their relationships—is to imply there is some ideal point at which all these things actually are fully developed, and the young person is considered incomplete until such a time. We are always in the process of developing. Our entire being is in constant flux from the moment we are born until the moment we die. If we are all constantly in a state of development (either progressive or regressive), then we have no cause for singling out the adolescent as the one who is undeveloped. Without denying the changes that do occur during the teen years, it is important that we learn to see young people as fully human right now.

The genesis of this undeveloped stereotype is our society's desire to control, understand, and predict everything. G.

Stanley Hall's work in the early twentieth century gave rise to the Child Study Movement. He built his work on Darwin's theory of evolution and modernity's assumption that human progress is inevitable. The foundational idea was that the development of the individual human must mimic the development of the species. Therefore, Hall and others began to equate early stages of an individual's development with earlier stages in the evolution of the human. Not only were children and adolescents assumed to correlate to less developed humans, so were women and minoritized people. The pinnacle of human development was the white male. Developmental psychology has since rejected these ideas and distanced itself from them. Yet, their influence remains.

Knowledge of these developmental pathways and milestones can be extremely helpful, especially when one's approach to education involves dividing young people into age groups. Knowing when a young person moves from concrete thinking to abstract thinking helps us organize children, schools, and lesson plans. Knowledge of these pathways is also helpful in that it enables us to notice when a young person is not developing at the "normal" pace (cognitively, socially, emotionally, physically, etc.) so that we can come alongside that young person with interventions necessary to help the young person thrive. Understanding the behavior considered to be normal for a certain age group goes a long way in helping us approach young people with empathy and patience.

Our use of developmental theory moves from helpful to harmful when our knowledge and relationship with a specific young person becomes defined less by knowing them for who they truly are and more by comparing them to what they are not. Such use is not the intention of developmental psychology's theories, but it is often the way these theories impact our work with young people. Developmental theories grew out of an assumption that we make adults the same way we make cars: on an assembly line. We founded our public-school system on this confident assumption that we can define how one can come to adulthood fully formed. Age-graded education made it necessary to know when a child masters certain skills and knowledge. We now know that young people do not all learn along the same trajectory, yet we still organize most of our schools this way. Developmental theories can be harmful when we misappropriate them as yardsticks for measuring how normal or abnormal a young person is. When my son and daughter go to visit their grandmother and she is unable to get her smart TV or DVD player to work, it is usually my fourteen-year-old son or my ten-year-old daughter who figures it out for her. In that situation, my kids are more developed than their seventy-two-year-old grandmother. Developmental theories are helpful in that they give us a descriptive snapshot of what could be. They are fairly dependent on the idea that there is a normal and an abnormal. But, really, are any of us normal? Such theories become harmful when we hold them up next to a specific young person as a measuring tool with the expectation that it can tell us exactly where she should be developmentally. To assume a young person is undeveloped is to blind yourself to their full humanity in the moment.

We do not need to look far in the church to see how this idea of young people as undeveloped has impacted our ministry with them. We have often divided Sunday schools by age. In congregations where this age-graded Sunday school is still functioning, it is not uncommon for congregations to have Sunday school during worship or to dismiss the young people during the sermon. The assumption is that the sermon is for those who are more developed, so those who are less developed need something different. Most committees or decision-making bodies in our congregations consist of adults, not young people. The assumption is that young people will be bored with a decision-making process or that they do not have the life experience to allow them insight into the decisions. The rallying cry of Young Life, one of the pioneer parachurch youth organizations, was "It's a sin to bore a kid." Such thoughts assume young people cannot handle the way adults spend their time in church and, therefore, need something wholly different. This is not an appeal to eliminate your congregation's unique ministries for young people, but it is an appeal to think deeply about the origins and assumptions of those ministries. Are they built upon assumptions of what your young people are fully capable of, or are they built upon assumptions of what they are not capable of?

> To assume a young person is undeveloped is to blind yourself to their full humanity in the moment.

Identity-less

We often attribute a young person's behavior to her perceived need to find herself. We think of the teenage years as the time of life when she must search for and discover her true identity. To be identity-less is to lack a deep sense of who you are or the life you wish to live. Many young people do feel this way. However, this does not mean they are without an identity and must go in search of one. The challenge for our young people is not to go find who they are but to discover and trust who they have always been.

The fear that we can be without an identity is based on a very modern understanding of the human that assumes the individual must search and find or create one's identity. Prior to the Enlightenment, your station in life and society was set at birth based on your parents' roles in society. Girls matured to be wives, mothers, and homemakers. Boys matured to take over their fathers' work as farmers, cobblers, noblemen, and so forth. The Enlightenment marked a new understanding of authority and the self. Our roots no longer determined our destinies. We could now create our own futures.

Prior to the Enlightenment, one did not need to search for one's identity. The presumed need to find oneself is a product of the Enlightenment. That is when we began talking about finding oneself as an external event of exploration and discovery. The Enlightenment's understanding of identity influenced psychologist Erik Erikson's popular theory of the eight stages of man. At each stage of life, we must resolve a crisis particular to that age before moving on to the subsequent age of development.[6]

According to Erikson's theory, adolescence is when we must resolve the crisis of identity. If a young person does not discover his true identity, then he succumbs to what Erikson calls role confusion and psychosis.[7] The young person suffers through this role confusion until he constructs a secure identity.

No other presumed characteristic of adolescence has shaped youth work as much as this notion of the search for identity. It has benefited our work with young people by opening our eyes to the value in building their self-confidence, helping them explore various life paths, and tapping into their full potential. In most cases, it is true that our roots no longer determine, or limit, our destinies. Therefore, it is important that we help young people explore and imagine the life they want to live. Yet, at the same time identity is not something we search for or construct. An overdependence on the externality and individuality of the search for identity, or the assumption that one is without an identity at any point in one's life, can have harmful results. One's identity is always forming and shifting, but no one is ever without a sense of identity. We should not define adolescence by the crisis of finding one's identity or the risk of not finding it. We always possess a true sense of self. Youth work is more about helping a young person realize who they already are than it is about helping them search for and discover who they might be.

Many congregations have built their youth ministries around this notion of the identity-less teenager. Just as we can think of adolescence as a technology, we can also think of ministry with young people as a technology. In this case, we hope the technology will help our young people find their identities. We purchase curricula, plan programs, schedule events, organize retreats, and take youth on trips that all promise to help our young people find their identities. So, here is the question: Is your congregation's ministry with young people built on the assumption you can help them search for and find their identity? Or, is it built upon the fact that they already are their true selves? There is a difference.

Self-Centered

The self-centered adolescent is as common a stereotype as the undeveloped adolescent. You know the one, walking through the mall, overly obsessed with what she is wearing while flashing a duck-face for the perfectly timed selfie. Even the term *selfie* encapsulates this idea of self-centeredness and has become a cultural phenomenon. It was *Oxford Dictionary*'s Word of the Year in 2013, and Scrabble officially added it in 2014.[8] We are quick to assume young people are self-absorbed and unable to consider anyone else's perspective or feelings. Yet, we all know young people who are incredibly selfless, and we all know the tendency toward self-centeredness is not unique to the teen years.

The assumption that young people are self-centered stems from a key finding in developmental psychology called *egocentrism*. Egocentrism exists in various forms across the lifespan. David Elkind was the first to focus on its presence during the adolescent years.[9] Egocentrism is the inability to distinguish between one's own perspective and the perspective of another.

For example, if a young person thinks she is ugly, she will assume all others around her think she is ugly as well.

It is wrong, however, to equate egocentrism with self-centeredness. They are not the same thing. We assume egocentrism is a deficiency, the inability to take another person's perspective, which causes us to equate it with self-centeredness. But egocentrism is not descriptive of a deficiency; it is descriptive of an emerging ability. It describes the tension caused by a young person's emerging ability to take another person's perspective. For the first time in their lives, teens can imagine what other people might be thinking about the world. It is a new, emerging skill for them, which they have not mastered. In fact, I am not sure we ever master it. It creates cognitive dissonance and a feedback loop as a young person tries to reconcile her own perception of herself with what she assumes to be someone else's perception of her. She is not self-centered. She is simply, for the moment, consumed by the cognitive work required to reconcile this feedback loop. Large crowds at a mall, football game, concert, or youth event only exacerbate the dissonance. Young people are not self-centered; they are learning to understand themselves in a complicated web of social relationships.

Identifying egocentrism with young people is both helpful and harmful. It helps us understand sources of real anxiety in a teenager's life, such as personal appearance, acceptance among peers, material possessions, too much attention, or not enough attention. It helps us understand their susceptibility to advertising, peer pressure, and bullying. The association of egocentrism, as self-centeredness, with adolescence has also been harmful.

It feeds our stereotype of the hoarding, materialistic, oblivious gluttony of adolescence. When a young person is in the throes of cognitive dissonance brought on by the merging of the internal and external perspectives of self and we interject with "Stop being so selfish," we only exacerbate the dissonance. The shame and shock force the young person either into her internal perception of herself or the perceived external perspective of her. She retreats into one or the other and does not learn how to balance the two. Behavior that appears as self-centered is not that at all. It is the normal behavior a young person exhibits when she is working to reconcile her own understanding of self with the world's understanding of her. I cannot think of an act that could be less self-centered.

Our ministries buy into this myth of self-centeredness when we present the Christian faith as primarily a personal relationship with Jesus. Christian faith is personal in that you are personally involved in it, but it never remains only personal. Christian faith is external and public. It is something lived out through actions in community. We sell-out to the myth of the self-centered adolescent when we assume we must discover and create programs and activities young people will like and choose to consume. Viewing egocentrism as a deficiency rather than an asset leads

> We sell-out to the myth of the self-centered adolescent when we assume we must discover and create programs and activities young people will like and choose to consume.

us to the assumption of self-centeredness. If we come to understand egocentrism for what it is, the emerging ability to think beyond one's own perspective, then we will invest less in programs and events and invest more into helping our young people reconcile the tension between their perception of the world and others' perceptions of the world.

Consumers

We also have a tendency to assume these self-centered, identityless, undeveloped adolescents care only about consuming products. We have reached a point as a society where it seems our primary purpose is to consume. If extraterrestrial beings were to visit our planet, it would not be farfetched for them to deduce that all we do is purchase, consume, and dispose. In my urban neighborhood, within one block of each other, there is a Target Greatland, a Walmart Supercenter, a Herberger's department store, and a Cub Foods. President George W. Bush encouraged Americans to shop and take trips to Disney World as ways of coping with the September 11 terrorist attacks and a slumping wartime economy.[10] Our young people are not immune to the cultural pressure to consume. It appears the only way we can imagine our young people contributing to society is through the role of consumer.

Advertising executives began to see young people as a target market not long after the rise of youth culture in the 1940s. *Seventeen* magazine was first published in 1944 and targeted young women in their teens. Youth culture was now distinct from adult culture and, therefore, required its own mechanisms of pollination. *Seventeen* and its competitors helped spread youth culture through their content and advertisements. These magazines knew "this year's purchaser of a poodle skirt would very likely be furnishing an entire household a year or two later."[11] They expected young people to develop brand loyalty not only toward poodle skirts and Benny Goodman but also toward ovens and laundry machines.

The push to consume has only increased over the years. There is disagreement in the world of marketing and communication on how many ads we process daily. So, without trying to quantify it scientifically, take a moment and think of all the times during the day you encounter either a brand name, logo, or an advertisement. Various messages constantly bombard us, vying for our money but also, ultimately, our attention and our loyalty. Now, imagine being a young person who is (a) repeatedly told you are undeveloped, (b) convinced you need to find your true identity, (c) trying to reconcile internal and external perceptions of yourself, and (d) simultaneously peppered with advertisements from corporations promising to provide you with that true identity.

This is the world our young people navigate. It is a world that convinces them their primary role is to consume and, through consumption, discover who they are. If you decide you are no longer a jock, then you purchase new music and new clothes and suddenly you have a new identity. Henry Giroux calls this the pedagogy of commodification and claims,

> The most consumer-oriented society in the world is fundamentally altering the very experiences and hopes of

young people, and often with tragic consequences. As Daniel Cook points out, "What is most troubling is that children's culture has become virtually indistinguishable from consumer culture over the course of the last century. The cultural marketplace is now a key arena for the formation of the sense of self and of peer relationships, so much so that parents often are stuck between giving into a kid's purchase demands or risking their child becoming an outcast on the playground."[12]

If one wants to respond to global terrorism, then one shops. If one wants to fit in with a social group, then one shops. If one wants to assert one's identity, then one shops.

Rather than challenging this dominate narrative of young people as consumers, the church has fallen prey to it. We struggle to liberate our young people from this death-dealing narrative of consumption and commodification, and instead, we come to see ourselves as a competitor in the marketplace of ideas and identities. We end up playing the consumption game, and religion becomes another product we try to sell to young people. Whether intentional or not, our strategy within the larger consumer context starts to sound as though we believe our young people must abandon the identity of youth hockey player or orchestra member to assume the identity of Christian teenager.

> Rather than challenging this dominate narrative of young people as consumers, the church has fallen prey to it.

We find ourselves competing for their time, competing for their loyalty, and sending the message that we are also competing for their identity.

Intersectionality and Disposability

We cannot discuss the challenges our young people face without discussing the reality of intersectionality. A culture that expects you to move through the world as an undeveloped consumer can place an even heavier burden upon you if you live at the intersection of various systems of oppression. We call this intersectionality. It describes the lived experience of people who—because of their race, class, gender, religion—find themselves experiencing different forms and degrees of oppression and -isms than others who may share one but not all of their social categorizations. For example, the way in which a young black woman experiences racism is different than the way a young black man experiences racism, and the way she experiences sexism is different than the way a young white woman experiences sexism. The adolescent, or the undeveloped consumer, is another layer of oppression placed upon those already living at the intersections. So, being a young person can be hard and oppressive. But being a young person of color or a young queer person or a young poor person is even more difficult. The oppression and bondage one experiences in a life lived as an undeveloped consumer experiencing intersectionality can seem insurmountable.

According to Henry Giroux, our society deems those young people who do not fit the mold of consumer as disposable.

Disposable youth are young persons who are either unable or unwilling to adopt the mantel of undeveloped consumer.[13] A young person living in poverty cannot participate in consumer culture at the same level as his peers across the country or, possibly, in his own community. He is disposable. He is unable to obtain the status of consumer. A young person with the means to participate in consumer culture but whose values do not align with that culture is disposable. He is unwilling to obtain this status. As we saw in the history of young people, our society can mobilize to make significant change for the sake of our economy but not always for the sake of our young people. So, herein lies the conundrum. Although it is dangerous to force our young people to fit the mold of the undeveloped consumer, it might be more dangerous for them if they do not fit.

There are significant biological and social changes that happen during the teen years. This life-stage we call adolescence is a very real thing. However, the adolescent is a myth. It is the stuff of B-grade movies. The adolescent is a mythical creature, a social construct that emerged from the convergence of a variety of societal shifts in the first half of the twentieth century. We can call this adolescent the undeveloped consumer because we mistakenly expect her to be an undeveloped, identity-less, self-centered consumer. In some ways, this is the role we need her to play in this society we have constructed—a necessary evil. So much so that we overlook young people who cannot fulfill this role and consider them disposable. Our call as Christian communities is to proclaim good news that liberates people from the bondage of their bad news. What might that good news sound like if the undeveloped consumer is the primary way in which our young people experience bondage? As we have seen in this chapter, many of our ministry practices are dependent upon and perpetuate this myth of the undeveloped consumer. The following chapters lay out an alternative way of seeing our young people that is liberating and life giving. Trust me, it gets better.

Discussion Questions

1. Take a moment to sit back and reminisce about your time as a teen. What were the stereotypes adults held of you and your peers at the time?
2. Who were the adults in your life who saw beyond these stereotypes and saw you for who you truly were? How did they do this?
3. How do the young people in your community surprise you and impress you?
4. Who are the disposable or vulnerable youth in your community? Who is advocating for them and with them?
5. Where in your community or in your congregation's ministry with young people do you see the residue of the undeveloped consumer? How might your ministry be perpetuating the myth of the undeveloped, self-centered, identity-less consumer?
6. How are your community and congregation currently liberating young people from this false identity of the undeveloped consumer?

2

Vocation as Liberation from the Undeveloped Consumer

For by grace you have been saved through faith, and this is not your own doing; it is the gift of God—not the result of works, so that no one may boast. For we are what he has made us, created in Christ Jesus for good works, which God prepared beforehand to be our way of life.

—Ephesians 2:8–10

I remember being frustrated as a teenager with adults' low expectations of my peers and me. We had good ideas, experiences, wisdom, and skills the church could use. In fact, we had gifts the entire community—our schools, neighborhoods, local

37

businesses, and so on—would have benefited from. The adults in our community rarely asked us to contribute. We were denied the opportunity to contribute through the good works that God had prepared beforehand to be our way of life. The same is true in many communities. Our dependence upon the myth of the adolescent, or the undeveloped consumer, prevents us from seeing the full potential in our young people. Christian theology and the biblical narrative offer us an alternative. There is no such thing as the undeveloped consumer in God's story. As we will see, it is best to understand our young people as those who are not undeveloped but called by God, not identity-less but named children of God, not self-centered but relational, and not consumers but cocreators with God in our world. God is calling them into this life. The framework of the called cocreator will liberate our young people from the dangerous myth of the undeveloped consumer.

A Biblical Understanding of Young People

So how does the myth of the undeveloped consumer hold up when we look at the Bible, both the Old Testament and the words of Jesus in the New Testament? The way Jesus talked about, received, and promoted young people provides motivation and material for deconstructing the undeveloped consumer. We will only understand how radical Jesus's embrace of young people was against the backdrop of the two worldviews shaping his life and teaching—Jewish theology and Greek philosophy. These were the two dominant worldviews in Jesus's life, and they both present different ways of understanding young people. Jesus moved beyond both perspectives and offered us a truly radical way of honoring our children and youth.[1] This biblical exploration will allow us to see how different Jesus's view of young people is from that which is common in our society today.

Let me add a quick word about life stages in Scripture. As I mention in chapter 1, the practice of dividing life into various stages of development is relatively new in the history of humanity. So, it should not surprise us that Scripture does not divide life into stages of development. The life stage we now call *adolescence* was not a reality in biblical times. You were either a child or you were an adult. Therefore, many of the passages in Scripture that refer to children are referring to younger children, not teens. We should naturally wonder if these verses addressing younger children are applicable to teens today. For example, in Matthew, Mark, and Luke, Jesus says, "Let the little children come to me." Can we use these words today as a call to welcome all young people including teens, or was Jesus only speaking of young children? I believe we can and we should. Jesus elevates children in Scripture because they are powerless, marginalized, and at risk. He is committed to those who are powerless, not those who fit into a specific age range. Over the course of history, we have infantilized, marginalized, and disempowered our teens.

> The life stage we now call *adolescence* was not a reality in biblical times. You were either a child or you were an adult.

Therefore, when Jesus elevates the powerless children in biblical times as exemplars of God's kingdom, I believe he is also lifting today's teens, who are also powerless and oppressed.

Young People in the Old Testament

Jesus's Holy Scriptures are what Christians refer to as the Old Testament. He was steeped in this worldview and its philosophy. The Old Testament consistently presents the young person as gift and responsibility. We are to cherish and tenaciously care for this gift, but we also have a responsibility to provide them with constant nurturing and protection. Walter Brueggemann draws on the Old Testament image of the she-bear to describe the tenacity with which we are to care for and protect our young people. Texts such as 2 Samuel 17:8, Proverbs 17:12, and Hosea 13:8 all use the phrase "like a she-bear robbed of her cubs" as a way of describing someone's righteous anger. The Hosea passage is speaking specifically of God's anger. According to these writers, nothing could be more angry or dangerous than a she-bear separated from her cubs. Brueggemann picks up on this metaphor and uses it to describe the passion with which God cares for God's children and the expectation God has for our care of our young people.[2]

Children are vulnerable and, therefore, requires our ferocious protection. Children also require nurturing. The Israelites understood the young person to be part of the covenant community. God acted in the lives of this community in a way that set this community apart as a chosen people for the sake of the world. "For the Lord your God dried up the waters of the Jordan for you until you crossed over, as the Lord your God did to the Red Sea, which he dried up for us until we crossed over, so that all the peoples of the earth may know that the hand of the Lord is mighty, and so that you may fear the Lord your God forever" (Josh 4:23–24).

Brueggemann points out how the pronouns change in this Joshua text. The text begins by speaking about *your* God who has done something for *you*. It then switches to say your God also did this thing for *us*. It then expands the reach of God's action to include *all the peoples of the earth*. The passage ends by returning to the *you* pronoun.[3] This shift in pronouns demonstrates the way Israelites believe young people are drawn into the covenant through God's action, not their own, and how that covenant becomes a blessing for all people of the earth. Young people are not outsiders who must earn a place within the covenant community; God draws them into the covenant for the sake of the world. Therefore, the larger covenant community is to take seriously the nurturing of the young people into the worldview and lifestyle of the covenant community.

Stephen Prothero describes Israel's understanding of human brokenness as life lived in exile.[4] Nurturing their young people into their covenant community is how the Israelite people resolve the problem of exile. Although God calls them to be God's covenantal community, they live life in suffering that comes from being in exile literally and metaphorically. The Jewish people are literally in exile, having experienced deportation and life without a country of their own for most of their history. They are figuratively in exile in that they are not living in relationship with God as God had intended. According to Prothero, we can understand Judaism's liberation as the return home to their promised land and to the promised relationship with God. Prothero goes on to explain how the Jewish community practices this return in two ways: through keeping the commandments and through telling their story. The covenant community nurtures and teaches a way of life shaped by the commandments and by the community's historical story. It is the community's top priority to nurture their young people into this covenant by teaching them the commandments and the story that shapes their lives. We see this commitment most clearly in Deuteronomy 6:4–9.

> Hear, O Israel: The Lord is our God, the Lord alone. You shall love the Lord your God with all your heart, and with all your soul, and with all your might. Keep these words that I am commanding you today in your heart. Recite them to your children and talk about them when you are at home and when you are away, when you lie down and when you rise. Bind them as a sign on your hand, fix them as an emblem on your forehead, and write them on the doorposts of your house and on your gates.

Young people are such a vital part of the community that adults are to nurture them intentionally in this covenant when they rise, when they lie down, when they are home, and when they are away.

God does not limit God's concern for young people to those who are members of Israel's covenant community. The Psalms and the prophets show God's love and concern extending to all children, especially orphans. Psalm 68:5 exalts God as the "Father of orphans." Isaiah calls Israel to "defend the orphan" (Isa 1:17). Jeremiah reminds Israel that God dwells with them when they are caring for the orphan (Jer 7:6–7). The psalmist sings of a God who "watches over the strangers; he upholds the orphan and the widow" (Ps 146:9). Because of God's actions, "the orphan ceases to be orphaned."[5] God's people, therefore, are to be as tenacious in defending and nurturing the orphan as they are their own young people.

> Young people are such a vital part of the community that adults are to nurture them intentionally in this covenant.

According to the Old Testament's witness, God sees young people as gift and responsibility. They are vulnerable, and we must tenaciously protect and defend them, especially the orphans. We are to nurture them in both the narrative and the lifestyle of the covenant people because God has already drawn them into the covenant community. God's investment in young people stretches far beyond those who are part of the inner circle and especially reaches those who are most vulnerable and marginalized.

Young People in Greek Thought and Culture

The ancient Greek understanding of the young person was quite different. Jesus would have also been familiar with this understanding of young people as he was born and raised in the Roman Empire and in a Palestinian world deeply influenced by Greek culture. Overall, the Greeks did not see young people as contributing members of society and culture. They were "fundamentally deficient and not yet human in the full sense."[6] Life as a young person in Greek culture was not valuable in and of itself. Rather, childhood was a training ground for adulthood that one must grow out of as soon as possible.[7] The Greeks did love their children and found great joy in parenthood. Yet, overall, young people were primarily economic and military necessities.[8] They would spend and make money and provide labor and military service to build the empire, but otherwise they occupied a very low position in Greek society. Judith Gundry-Volf claims their social status was comparable to that of slaves.[9] The young person of Greek culture begins to sound like the young person (the undeveloped consumer) of our own culture.

Young People in the New Testament

Again, Jesus would have been familiar with and influenced by both the Old Testament's teachings on young people and Greek culture's view of young people. They were the dominant, and conflicting, worldviews of his time. The way Jesus interacts with young people and speaks of them in the New Testament turns the Greek understanding on its head and makes the

44

Jewish understanding even more potent. Gundry-Volf high-lights five ways Jesus addresses and practices the significance of young people.[10]

1. Jesus presents young people as *recipients of the reign of God*. In Mark 10:13–16, Jesus scolds his disciples for preventing the children from coming to him and tells them that God's kingdom belongs to these children.

2. In the same text, we see Jesus pointing to young people as *exemplars of how to live into God's kingdom*. He says God's kingdom belongs to these children, and if anyone wishes to enter it, they must receive it as these children do.

3. Jesus also implores his disciples to learn from the young peoples' *example of humility*. In Matthew 18:1–5, Jesus's disciples are asking him who will be the greatest in heaven. Jesus places a young person in their midst and says, "Whoever becomes humble like this child is the greatest in the kingdom of heaven" (Matt 18:4).

4. Jesus continues teaching his disciples, "Whoever welcomes one such child in my name welcomes me" (Matt 18:5). Not only are young people examples of humility, they are also *conduits for Christ's presence*. If we welcome young people into our midst, we are welcoming Jesus as well.

5. Jesus also contrasts young people with the scribes and Pharisees as *having true insight into Jesus's divine nature*. The scribes and Pharisees were the most learned leaders within Judaism. They are the ones who best understood

God's word and God's law. However, when they become angry with a group of young people for praising Jesus after healing a blind man, Jesus says to them, "Out of the mouths of infants and nursing babies you have prepared praise for yourself" (Matt 21:16). In saying this, he showcases these young people as having special insight into Jesus's identity and mission.

Gundry-Volf also shows us how Paul's letters address (or fail to address) young people. Unfortunately, Paul's letters lose Jesus's radical embrace of young people as exemplars. A child of believing parents is holy but is not an exemplar. Most of Paul's writing about children is only in relation to family codes. Bonnie Miller-McLemore claims these family codes of Ephesians 5:22–6:9 and Colossians 3:18–4:1 "reassert conventional patriarchal family structures," which seem to contradict the way Jesus and "the gospel narrative [challenge] the usual norms of social status and [demand] stunning respect for children."[11] Although Paul's letters mention children as part of the family unit, they seem to lose Jesus's potent embrace of young people and to succumb to the traditional Jewish teachings and especially to Greek culture. From Jesus's perspective, the children are far more than slaves or even vulnerable

> Young people embody tangible ways we can welcome Jesus into our midst, and they possess inspired insight into who Jesus truly is.

members of the covenant community. They are exemplars who have received God's kingdom and can teach us how to receive it as well. Young people embody tangible ways we can welcome Jesus into our midst, and they possess inspired insight into who Jesus truly is. Jesus implores us to see our young people as blessed models of greatness within God's reign.

Clearly there is no equivalence between Jesus's vision of young people and the undeveloped consumer. Rather than being undeveloped, Jesus sees them as being fully capable in the present moment to respond to God's call as exemplars of life in the reign of God. Rather than being identity-less, we see Jesus welcome them into his arms and bless them just as the Israelites saw God drawing the young people into the covenant community. They are not without an identity but are made aware of their given identity, child of God. Rather than being self-centered, we clearly hear Jesus praise young people for their humility and selflessness. Rather than young people existing as consumers, we see these young people as agents, conduits of God's presence, and cocreators of God's kingdom on earth. While undeveloped, identity-less, self-centered consumers might describe how young people react to and present themselves within Western culture, they do not describe God's vision and hope for our young people. Our young people seem to be in bondage to these low expectations we have of them. If we are to proclaim good news that liberates them from this bondage, then we will need to reacquaint ourselves with Christ's vision for young people and Christ's call to young people.

What Is Vocation?

Jesus's vision for our young people is a vocational understanding of young people. *Vocation*, as a term, can be used in many ways. Sometimes it refers to our jobs. Other times it refers to vocational/technical schools you attend for a two-year specialized degree in certain fields such as pipe fitting, x-ray technician, or computer programming. Some still use it to differentiate church professions from work outside the church. The word vocation derives from the Latin word *vocare*, which means to call or summon. Therefore, vocation and calling are interchangeable terms. I prefer to use the term *vocation* to renew our interest in it. This complex word holds an important place in our work with young people as it helps us address some of the threats to their well-being we have covered thus far.

To begin to appreciate what vocation means in the fullest sense and how it will be used here, we first must understand the historical context in which Martin Luther's doctrine of vocation emerged and where this doctrine fits within Luther's theological system.[12] It will also be necessary to explore some critiques of Luther's doctrine of vocation. In the end, it will become clear that vocation is a powerful theological tool that holds great promise for us as we seek to dismantle the undeveloped consumer and offer a more life-giving alternative.

Vocation as a Product of Martin Luther's Historical Context

In 1517, Martin Luther famously posted the Ninety-Five Theses outlining his grievances against the Roman Catholic Church's sale of indulgences. Luther and his colleagues quickly mass-produced this document and spread it across Germany. The church had been practicing the distribution of indulgences for some time. An indulgence was a piece of paper recognizing and certifying one's completion of a particular good work. A priest would assign good works to a believer after the believer had completed confession with his priest. An indulgence was "proof" of the completion of the good work and, therefore, a guarantee that punishment for the sin confessed would be withheld. Donations to the church soon became one of the common good works assigned to believers. By Luther's time, this evolved into the full-blown commercialization of forgiveness through the sale of indulgences. An individual could now purchase forgiveness or even the forgiveness of relatives who had already passed. Luther's study of Scripture showed him that forgiveness only comes to the sinner through the grace of God, and not through our good works. The church was taking advantage of peoples' fear of death and damnation to increase its revenue.

Luther's epiphany of God's free grace also led him to realize the universality of vocation. At Luther's time, society considered only those who served the church to have vocations. The church leaders were the only ones to have special calls from God. It was through the calls of these church leaders that others would have access to God and, ultimately, salvation. But Luther's understanding of God's grace given freely opened his eyes to the falseness of this teaching as well. God's grace is given freely by God. Therefore, priests, monks, cardinals, and bishops are not the only ones who can do God's work in the world. They are not the only ones who can read, interpret, or proclaim God's word. Vocation does not take place between God and humans; only God works in that space. Rather, vocation for Luther takes place between our neighbor and ourselves. Therefore, God calls everyone to do God's work through serving their neighbor for their neighbor's sake, not for God's sake or for the church's sake. Luther's famous formula for vocation was, "A Christian is lord of all, completely free of everything. A Christian is a servant, completely attentive to the needs of all."[13] Luther would say that Christ has freed us so we are no longer in bondage to anything or anyone, yet at the same time we have been freed for service to our neighbor. It is freedom because it is done out of joy for this life rather than out of fear of God or death.

Vocation in the Context of Martin Luther's Theology

We also gain a better understanding of Luther's doctrine of vocation when we look at how it fits within his entire theological system. This project does not allow me to give the fullness of Luther's theology the space and time it deserves. However, it is important to attempt to summarize his theology. Figure 2 will provide us with a helpful, albeit limited, visual as we piece Luther's theology together to grasp his understanding of vocation.[14]

For Luther, life happens within two overlapping realms, the heavenly realm and the earthly realm. The Christian exists within these two realms simultaneously. You can see these two realms listed in figure 2. We live our lives relationally in both

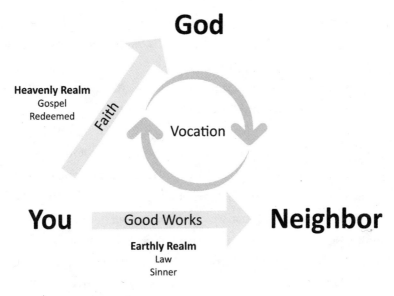

Figure 2: Diagram of Luther's Theology

realms. We sometimes refer to these relationships as the vertical relationship with God in the heavenly realm and the horizontal relationship with our neighbor in the earthly realm. God defines these relationships with love. The arrows moving from you to neighbor and to God represent this love. In the vertical relationship of the heavenly realm, the way we love God is through our faith. We trust God. In the horizontal relationship of the earthly realm, the way we love our neighbor is through good works. We serve our neighbor. According to Luther, we live as sinners and redeemed simultaneously. We never become more or less of one or the other. Luther also understood God's work to function differently in these two realms. In the heavenly realm, it is God's work of the gospel that redeems us and enables us to have faith in and trust God. In the earthly realm, it is God's law that confronts us as sinners and compels us to have concern for our neighbor's well-being.

The circular arrows represent vocation. It is the life we live at the intersections of the heavenly and earthly, redemption and sin, gospel and law, faith and good works. God continues God's creative work in our world through our vocations. God has no need of our good works in the heavenly realm, but our neighbors do in the earthly realm. God frees us from the desire to serve God and ourselves so that we can turn and serve our neighbor. God desires God's people to have a future and an abundant life. God ensures our future through God's law, but we no longer encounter God's law as law once the gospel has freed us. We now receive it as God's divine mandate or command, and "what the command means depends on each [person]'s living neighbor and his varying needs. Since it is in my situation on earth that I meet my neighbor, my vocation comprehends all my relations with different 'neighbors'; indeed, my vocation can be said to consist of those relations."[15] This vocational understanding of what it means to be human gives us ground to stand upon as we challenge the undeveloped consumer.

Potential Dangers of Vocation

Just like a dusty country road, vocation has two ditches we can fall into when attempting to explain it. One ditch makes vocation sound complacent and oppressive. A group of scholars, initiated by the Lilly Endowment's Programs for the Theological

Exploration of Vocation Grant, have being working for years with young people around the idea of vocation through college and seminary hosted vocation and theology institutes for youth.[16] Some of these scholars have offered a helpful critique of vocation's potential for oppression and complacency. David White points out the danger of Luther's emphasis upon stations when developing his doctrine of vocation.[17] According to Luther, every individual is born into a station through which they can do God's work by fulfilling the duties of those stations. These stations would include our social status and roles—peasant, laborer, father, wife. However, White highlights Luther's lack of a critical perspective on the oppressive nature of these stations. The laborer, in Luther's thought, was to be grateful for his station in life and fulfill his duties with joy in knowing he is doing God's work in the world. The laborer was not to question the inadequacy of his pay, nor was he to aspire to anything greater. Luther's intent was to bring honor and meaning to positions often considered to be lowly and meaningless. He desired everyone to know they could do God's work just as faithfully as a priest or the pope. At Luther's time, life lived in stations was the common and unquestioned worldview. However, in our time this emphasis upon stations can be, and has been, "used to justify slavery and the subjugation of women."[18]

The emphasis on stations can also translate into complacency or quietism in our day. It expects the marginalized and powerless to find meaning and purpose in their place in society. Simultaneously, vocation runs the risk of lulling those with power and privilege to sleep. It can cause us to take an ahistorical perspective on current social problems. For example, the barrage of police shootings of African American men has left our country divided between Black Lives Matter and Blue Lives Matter. If we naively transfer Luther's justification of stations from his time to our time, which many do, it becomes quite easy to chalk up these deaths to unfortunate consequences of police just trying to do their jobs. Such a perspective is an ahistorical look at the problem that does not take into consideration the centuries of oppression and exploitation of black and brown bodies by the dominant white society. Therefore, David White encourages congregations to tap into "youthful idealism" as a modern incarnation of the Hebrew prophets.[19]

Dori Grinenko Baker and Joyce Ann Mercer hope our young people will embrace the roles of "prophets, sages, healers, and activists who will sense an urgent call, find a community of support, and respond with lives to offer."[20] They rightfully critique the potential of Luther's doctrine of vocation (especially its dependence upon stations) to allow those who are in power to remain in power without questioning how they received this power and why others are forced to live without the same power and privilege.

However, Baker, Mercer, and White come close to falling into the other ditch. In this second ditch, vocation becomes determined by a heroic agenda. For example, Baker and Mercer's hope for prophets, sages, healers, and activists is optimistic and commendable. However, these are heroic roles to fill. White is correct to view a young person's idealism as a gift. But if we only talk about vocation as a call to these heroic roles, then we run the risk of teaching our young people to overlook the ordinary and mundane ways to do God's work in service to the neighbor daily. Vocation is one's call to serve the neighbor for the neighbor's sake. That neighbor might need a prophetic voice or wisdom or healing or an activist and advocate. Or that neighbor might just need a friend, a warm meal, or for us to leave them the heck alone. Luther says, "we should be guided in all our works by this one thought alone—that we may serve and benefit others in everything that is done, having nothing else before our eyes except the need and advantage of the neighbor."[21] There is no heroic agenda behind vocation, though vocation might be heroic. The neighbor is the agenda as she places specific demands upon me at a certain time and location. We must avoid the ditch of complacent quietism, but we also must avoid the ditch of heroic agendas. The avoidance of these two ditches, or dangers of vocation, will be critical as we move forward. Both can be detrimental to the well-being of our young people.

> Vocation is one's call to serve the neighbor for the neighbor's sake.

Vocation Is . . .

The concept of vocation is not without its difficulties and potential pitfalls. However, I hope you are beginning to see its urgency and effectiveness for reframing our understanding of young people. In summary, I offer these six points that highlight key aspects of vocation. These points will serve as important hand-holds as we move forward on this journey.

Vocation Is Freedom

Our young people—and all of us, for that matter—have been set free from anxious attempts to justify ourselves through achievements and good works and are therefore set free for works that are done in response to our neighbors' actual needs rather than for our need for self-justification. When attempting to define vocation, it is wise to begin with Luther's two-fold thesis as mentioned earlier, "A Christian is lord of all, completely free of everything. A Christian is a servant, completely attentive to the needs of all."[22] This thesis is rooted in Luther's interpretation of 1 Corinthians 9:19, in which Paul proclaims, "For though I am free with respect to all, I have made myself a slave to all." Vocation is the life to which God calls us and for which Christ has set us free. It is a freedom that maintains the unity between Ephesians 2:8–9 and Ephesians 2:10 as seen at the beginning of this chapter. Faith saves us, not works, and this frees us to perform the good works we were intended to perform since creation.

Vocation Is Relational

Luther rejects an autonomous view of the human self and instead opts for a relational understanding of the human that recognizes the reality of human community and our need to care for one another. Vocation happens not in a vacuum but within the context of a community, in a world with deep needs, and through a variety of relationships with (sometimes conflicting) demands. The freedom of vocation draws our young people deeply into relationships.

Vocation Is Spontaneous

Because vocation is relational, it is also spontaneous. According to Luther, we cannot move through life with a list of criteria that distinguishes good works from bad works, or significant works from insignificant works. Gustaf Wingren explicitly names the neighbor as "the center of Luther's ethics, not God's kingdom or God's law or 'character.'"[23] A young person's call to serve the neighbor will take shape in different ways depending upon the immediate needs of her neighbor, not on her own idea of what the neighbor needs—no matter how compassionate her own idea might be. The "spontaneous love" of vocation prevents a certain type of dehumanizing that can happen when one population assumes it has the solution to another population's tribulation.[24]

Vocation Is Ordinary

Because vocation is spontaneous, it is also ordinary. It is not uncommon for a person to equate the word vocation with career or job. While a job might reflect one's particular voca-tion, a vocation is far more than a job. It is also far more than profound acts of kindness, charity, or justice. The relational con-text of vocation and spontaneity that comes with freedom in

these relationships both lead to a certain ordinariness of vocation. One does not need to sell all her belongings and move to
an orphanage halfway around the world to live out a vocation.
Instead, it happens in our day-to-day lives as parents, siblings,
neighbors, students, coworkers, friends, and employees. It is in
this daily ordinariness that our lives reach out beyond themselves as proclamations of hope.[25]

Vocation Is Here and Now

Because vocation is ordinary, it is also here and now. Vocation
happens, and it happens now. We often speak of vocation as
something one must find or discover before it is too late, because
we often equate vocation with a job. Vocation is freedom, relational, spontaneous, and ordinary. When we define vocation
internally, as though it only has to do with our gifts and interests,
we relegate vocation to the future. However, when we define
vocation externally, as taking place within relationships, vocation quickly becomes something of the present. Wingren urges
us not to "rack [our] brains about the future, but to live in the
hour that has come. That is the same as living in faith, receptive
to God, who is present now."[26] As long as our young people have
a neighbor, they have a vocation.

Vocation Is God's Presence and Activity

Wingren minces no words: "This view of vocation cannot be
emphasized enough. Through vocation God's presence is really

with [humankind]."[27] As you will see below, young people use vocational language to describe moments when God was particularly present and active in their lives. They describe moments in nature when they experienced a sense of smallness, which increased or deepened their awareness of their dependence on God. They describe service experiences in which views toward a certain population transformed as they discovered their mutual humanity and responsibility for one another. They talk about other experiences that resulted in a heightened sense of responsibility for protecting nature. Their descriptions of these experiences seem to support Wingren's claim; vocation is how God is present among us.

How Does Vocation Liberate Young People?

Not only is vocation an important building block for constructing an alternative to the undeveloped consumer, it is also the chosen theological category used by young people when they describe how God is at work in their lives. I had the privilege of interviewing teenagers around the country while conducting research for my dissertation. I was exploring the way they made sense of what they considered to be experiences of God's presence and activity in their lives. This study concluded with the claim that our young people do not talk about encountering God

God is working to liberate them from the undeveloped consumer by awakening them to the fullness of their vocation.

through salvation-type experiences, rather they describe their encounters with God as vocational experiences—calls into deeper dependence upon God, calls into stewardship of creation, and calls into responsibility toward one's neighbor.[28] Through their stories, we can see how God is working to liberate them from the undeveloped consumer by awakening them to the fullness of their vocation.

Vocation Awakens Dependence upon God

Sarah, a seventeen-year-old in Seattle, described experiencing the presence and activity of God in a moment when she became more deeply aware of her dependence upon God. Living in Seattle, she often does not see the stars at night. The cloud cover and lights from the city mask them almost nightly. She saw the Milky Way for the first time in her life on a weekend retreat into the Cascade Mountains. She became acutely aware of the vastness of the cosmos and the smallness of her own life. It was both terrifying and comforting for her to see the expanse of God's work while also knowing the particularity of God's love in her own life. She now sees this same God who created this vast cosmos is also animating her life.

Vocation Awakens Stewardship of Creation

Another young woman, tenth-grader Krystal, described her emerging sense of call to care for God's creation. Her family lives on a body of water. She regularly climbs out her bedroom window to sit on the roof of the house and take in the view and the smells. Those are the moments she decided to share with me as moments when God is particularly present and active. She said she senses God calling her to care for creation through the smell of the sun on the pine trees. Isn't that beautiful!

Vocation Awakens Responsibility to the Neighbor

Jakob, an eleventh-grader in a midwestern suburb, spent most of his interview telling me how no one in his school liked him or understood him. He always felt like the outsider and only found enjoyment in video games. One Saturday, his pastor invited him to come with her to volunteer at a downtown shelter for those experiencing homelessness. He did not want to go, but he went along. Jakob enjoyed his time and found those living in the shelter to be great people. In fact, after spending much time telling me how he did not fit in anywhere, he said "I really connected with those people . . . they were so excited to have us there . . . I felt like a special person."[29] He described an experience in which he was both called out of himself to serve the neighbor and simultaneously received and accepted in a way he had never been before. In this moment, he gained a stronger sense of his responsibility to his neighbor, and he explained this moment as a time and place in which God was present and active.

These are just a few examples of how vocation is freedom, relational, spontaneous, ordinary, present tense, and the location of God's activity and presence. These are also examples of how our young people experience liberation through vocation.

I heard many stories like these. These are not stories of undeveloped, selfish, identity-less consumers. Our young people feel trapped by this myth of the undeveloped consumer. It is no wonder that when asked to describe moments in their lives when God is at work, they chose moments in which God was liberating them from that myth. Jesus calls our young people into dependence upon God, stewardship of creation, and responsibility for the neighbor. He has always seen young people as having this call. We are not talking about future potential; we are talking about present-moment reality. Vocation is the theological building block we need to construct a powerful antidote to the myth of the undeveloped consumer.

Vocation of the Called Cocreator

As we have seen, Christian theology and the biblical narrative offer a viable alternative to the undeveloped consumer. The undeveloped-consumer framework views young people as undeveloped, while the called-cocreator framework views them as called, in this moment. An undeveloped consumer is in search of an elusive identity, whereas, by contrast, a called cocreator knows she is a child of God. The undeveloped consumer is only concerned with meeting his own personal needs, but the called cocreator approaches life relationally. Lastly, the undeveloped consumer understands her vocation to be consumer of goods. The called cocreator knows God calls her to be a cocreator of God's world. The next four chapters will show how our young people are already called, children of God, relational, and cocreators. This framework can reinvigorate our ministry with young people and liberate them—and us—from the undeveloped consumer.

Discussion Questions

1. Review the biblical texts used to construct a biblical understanding of young people in the first part of this chapter. Which one resonates with you and the way you desire to "see" young people the most? Why?

2. Review the five ways Jesus addresses and practices the significance of young people according to Gundry-Volf on pp. 45–46. How do these affirm or challenge your congregation's current ministry with young people?

3. Write out, in your own words and in language the young people of your congregation would understand, a definition of *vocation* discussed in this chapter. Discuss your definitions and explain why this is important.

4. Describe a time when you experienced God calling you.

5. How do you currently see the young people in your congregation discerning their calls? How can your congregation support them in this work? How can your congregation help them recognize those experiences as God working to liberate them?

3

Called

¹Now the boy Samuel was ministering to the Lord under Eli. The word of the Lord was rare in those days; visions were not widespread. ²At that time Eli, whose eyesight had begun to grow dim so that he could not see, was lying down in his room; ³the lamp of God had not yet gone out, and Samuel was lying down in the temple of the Lord, where the ark of God was. ⁴Then the Lord called, "Samuel! Samuel!" and he said, "Here I am!" ⁵and ran to Eli, and said, "Here I am, for you called me." But he said, "I did not call; lie down again." So he went and lay down. ⁶The Lord called again, "Samuel!" Samuel got up and went to Eli, and said, "Here I am, for you called me." But he said, "I did not call, my son; lie down again." ⁷Now Samuel did not yet know the Lord, and the word of the Lord had not yet been revealed to him. ⁸The Lord called Samuel again, a third time. And he got up and went to Eli, and said, "Here I am, for you called me." Then Eli perceived that the Lord was calling the

boy. [9]Therefore Eli said to Samuel, "Go, lie down; and if he calls you, you shall say, 'Speak, Lord, for your servant is listening.'" So Samuel went and lay down in his place.

[10]Now the Lord came and stood there, calling as before, "Samuel! Samuel!" And Samuel said, "Speak, for your servant is listening." [11]Then the Lord said to Samuel, "See, I am about to do something in Israel that will make both ears of anyone who hears of it tingle. [12]On that day I will fulfill against Eli all that I have spoken concerning his house, from beginning to end. [13]For I have told him that I am about to punish his house forever, for the iniquity that he knew, because his sons were blaspheming God, and he did not restrain them. [14]Therefore I swear to the house of Eli that the iniquity of Eli's house shall not be expiated by sacrifice or offering forever."

[15]Samuel lay there until morning; then he opened the doors of the house of the Lord. Samuel was afraid to tell the vision to Eli. [16]But Eli called Samuel and said, "Samuel, my son." He said, "Here I am." [17]Eli said, "What was it that he told you? Do not hide it from me. May God do so to you and more also, if you hide anything from me of all that he told you." [18]So Samuel told him everything and hid nothing from him. Then he said, "It is the Lord; let him do what seems good to him." [19]As Samuel grew up, the Lord was with him and let none of his words fall to the ground.

—1 Samuel 3:1–19

Multiple examples throughout Scripture show God calling young people to play significant roles in the narrative arc of justice and salvation, including Samuel (above), David (1 Sam 16:1–13), Jeremiah (Jer 1:4–10), and Mary (Luke 1:26–38). Samuel's story, however, seems to offer us the best insight into the potency of these calls. The verses above are rich in imagery as they describe the context of Samuel's call.

In the text, God's word and visions are rare, and Eli struggles with sight, but the lamp of God had not yet gone out. There is hope. Eli cannot see, but he can hear. Samuel's hearing seems to be off, so Eli must help him understand what he is hearing. Eli teaches Samuel how to respond to the call from God; God promises God's actions will make ears tingle. The words Samuel receives from God for Eli will not be good news to Eli; they will be judgment. Eli seems to expect this, but he still coaches Samuel through the call process.

Samuel's mother wanted him to be a priest like Eli. Eli knows God is calling Samuel into prophecy, even if the words Samuel delivers from God to Eli are those of judgment. No one, except God, was expecting this for Samuel. God calls the young ones. The older ones must accept this and teach them to hear and respond to the call of God, even if that means the young ones will point out our flaws. This is the level of commitment it takes if we truly believe God is calling our young people. In the end, none of their words will fall to the ground; rather they will make our ears tingle.

Called versus Undeveloped

The undeveloped consumer framework leads us to believe our young people have not yet fully arrived or are not yet fully human. This belief makes it difficult for us to imagine God actually calling young people and working through them for the sake of our world. The theologically informed framework of the called cocreator, however, believes God is calling each person to join in God's work at this very moment. God is not waiting until our brains, bodies, or social capacities are fully formed. God calls every one of us into service today, in this moment. Therefore, we make the bold claim that everyone has a call, or vocation, from God to serve their neighbors in their daily lives. We fulfill this call through our relationships—whether neighbor, classmate, teammate, son, daughter, partner, spouse, or coworker. To be called means we are set free to partner with God in the healing of the world for the sake of the world, not to earn God's favor. Our young people have this call now; it is not something they have to wait for adulthood to live.

> God is calling each person to join in God's work at this very moment.

The following ten points will give us more insight into what it means to be called by God, to have a vocation, and how this is radically different than being somewhere below completion on a developmental trajectory. Each thesis merits its own book, so this is just the tip of the iceberg, but it will begin to frame the urgency of this perspective for our work with young people. What follows is a description of each thesis, some examples to help you better understand its claim, and some discussion about why this claim is important for our young people. Labeling our young people as *undeveloped* places them in bondage to our low expectations. Reminding them that God is calling them into a life of service liberates them for the life God has in store for them.

The Call Comes from Outside of You

A call is a gift given to you from beyond yourself. A call is not something that grows within you. Your own awareness of it might grow within you, but the call comes from outside of you. The undeveloped consumer is undeveloped because that which is internal does not quite measure up to an external, socially constructed idea of normal development. We compare the individual to the universal. The called cocreator is called because the external, universal call from God is a gift to the individual.

The story of Samuel's call refers to Samuel as "the boy Samuel." Most biblical scholars believe he was probably twelve years old. Samuel's mother had brought him to Eli so that Eli might train Samuel to be a priest. It is, therefore, safe to assume he was developmentally ready to begin priestly training. Neither his mother nor Eli assumed he was ready to be a prophet; at least not until the call came from God—from outside Samuel. His call did not well up inside him. It came from beyond.

Chapter 2 introduced us to Krystal and her call to care for creation. Her call to be a steward of God's creation did not come from within her. It came from beyond her, riding on the scent of the pine trees. One's call is not dependent upon one's internal developmental phase. It is dependent upon the external gifting of the call from God to the individual.

To Be Called Implies a Caller

Because the call comes from beyond us, and does not grow within us, it implies a caller. Our young people are not just called, they are called by God. They do not make up or imagine their calls. God gives these calls. There is no caller necessary in the world of the undeveloped consumer. The only thing necessary to uphold its framework is a universal, socially constructed norm against which we compare and judge our young people.

Samuel knew there was a caller. He mistakenly assumed it was Eli. Yet, he still knew this external call was coming from someone. The word of God and visions were both rare. Yet, Samuel knew his call was originating from someone he should seek.

We hear more about this caller in Luke's account of the annunciation. When God calls Mary to bear Christ on behalf of humanity, she asks the angel Gabriel how this could be. Gabriel replies, "The Holy Spirit will come upon you, and the power of the Most High will overshadow you" (Luke 1:35a). The Greek word translated as "overshadow" is *episkiazo*, which is used only one other time in the New Testament. It appears in the story of the transfiguration when Peter is pleading to build tents for Jesus, Moses, and Elijah so they can stay on the mountain. "A cloud came and *overshadowed* them . . . then from the cloud came a voice that said, 'This is my son; my Chosen; Listen to him!'" (Luke 9:34–35). When we base our understanding of our call on our desires alone, we run the risk of allowing ourselves to be mis- led. It is good news that our own desires become overshadowed by God's desires. A call without a caller cannot free us from the limits of our own desires. God, the caller beyond the one called, overshadows our young people and their expectations.

> A call without
> a caller cannot
> free us from
> the limits of our
> own desires.

The Caller Desires the Called

God, the caller, gifts each young person with the call. God does this because God desires each young person. God desires they learn to follow God, to live into the life God has for them. God desires that they partner with God in the healing of this world. The Christian narrative stakes its claim on a relational, Trinitar- ian understanding of God. Because God is Trinitarian, three in one, then God is a relationship. Our relational God desires to be in a relationship with God's creation. God calls our young peo- ple because God desires a relationship with them. There is noth- ing about the undeveloped consumer that implies being desired by anything other than an impersonal society that expects him to achieve full developmental normalcy in order to begin contrib- uting to society through consumption.

We see the caller desiring the called when God says to Jeremiah, "Before I formed you in the womb I knew you" (Jer 1:5a). We see it in Mary's call when Gabriel addresses her as the "favored one" (Luke 1:28b). These are not the abstract calls of a distant caller to no one in particular. These are intimate calls of a personal God to people who are clearly known by God.

When Sarah encountered the Milky Way for the first time in her life (as described in chapter 2) she encountered the *limitlessness* of God's love for a vast cosmos. Yet, she also encountered the *specificity* of God's love for her, a tiny piece of this vast cosmos. In that experience of hearing God's call, Sarah felt known and desired by God.

Jakob encounters God's desire for him in the homeless peoples' desire to know Jakob and spend time with him. Jakob clearly sensed that not many people seemed to desire his company. His perception changed when he experienced those who are homeless desiring to know him. Jakob understood this to be an encounter with God's presence and God's desire.

The Called Person Is Equipped for the Call Right Now

Samuel's inability to see that it was God calling him did not prevent God from calling him. God calls each young person to participate in God's work right now. God would not call them to this work if God was not able to equip them. They are ready right now. They will be ready to answer the call in a new way tomorrow and each day after. But they are also fully ready right now. On the other hand, the undeveloped consumer cannot be fully ready until she has completely developed, which is never. To be called is to be made ready in the moment, for the moment.

Martha is an ordained pastor in the Evangelical Lutheran Church in America. She is an active leader in her synod's environmental stewardship work. Her radical commitment to care for and protect God's creation comes across regularly in her preaching and teaching. When Martha was fifteen years old, she was a peer minister in my congregation's youth ministry. Our adult leaders and peer ministers would meet monthly to discern the next steps for our ministry together. At one of these meetings, Martha expressed her concern about the amount of garbage we produced each Sunday when our senior-high students gathered for dinner before their small groups. She was certain God would prefer us using and washing real dishes rather than filling two huge garbage bags with Styrofoam and plastic each week. The adults, including myself, worried the dishwashing process would cut into too much small-group time. Martha was adamant and asked, "Why couldn't a different small group wash dishes each week and just meet while they washed?" Our group of leaders looked at one another and agreed this made a lot of sense. We implemented it the next week. At the end of the year, the leaders said some of their best conversations happened while washing dishes. Martha was, and is, called by God to care for God's creation. She was

> Our young people do not need to wait to respond to God's call. They are prepared and equipped to respond right now.

prepared for that work as a fifteen-year-old. She is prepared for that work in new ways as a thirty-year-old. Our young people do not need to wait to respond to God's call. They are prepared and equipped to respond right now.

The Call Is an Invitation, Not a Plan

It is dangerous to speak of God's call as a plan. The nomenclature of *plan* brings with it the expectations of a clear and obvious predetermined pathway. God's call is rarely obvious or predetermined. God's call is an invitation to follow, but it is not a blueprint or map of the pathway the journey will take. The framework of the undeveloped consumer is dependent upon a blueprint that judges each young person based on where he is currently located along the way. God's call is not about progress but rather about relationships, trust, and putting one foot forward (or backward) at a time as we struggle to live the life of discipleship.

"For surely I know the plans I have for you, says the Lord, plans for your welfare and not for harm, to give you a future with hope" (Jer 29:11). We often cite these words from Jeremiah's letter to the Israelites in exile to prove or reassure someone that God has their best interest in mind. But what God is offering the Israelites is hardly a plan. Rather, it is a set of promises and an invitation to live into them. There is no premarked pathway or prediction, only a promise. The "you" in this verse is also plural, not singular. God extends these promises and invitation to us collectively, not to us as individuals.

I met Rob when he was a nineteen-year-old freshman at Augsburg University enrolled in one of the courses I was teaching. Rob introduced himself on the first day of class as an addict in recovery from both drug and alcohol addiction. Rob had come to a point in his recovery where he was eager to put his trust in a higher power, but he was not yet willing to call this higher power anything specific such as Yahweh, Brahman, Allah, God, or Jesus. Yet, he was absolutely certain this higher power was calling him to a better life of sobriety. Rob did not know what that was going to look like in the near or distant future. There was no clear plan in his mind. He was, however, certain sobriety would define the journey. Rob's call was an invitation into a continuously unfolding life of sobriety, but it contained no specific plan.

The Call Is for the Common Good

In his first letter to the church at Corinth, Paul is begging the Corinthians to recognize the variety of gifts within the larger community. He wants them to know God's spirit has given them a variety of gifts that are very different from one another, but all these gifts matter to the well-being of the body of Christ. Each gift is unique, but each gift is the same in that each gift given is for the common good (1 Cor 12:7). Our young peoples' calls and gifts are not for their own betterment or development. Their calls are for the common good.

In 2012, the local NBC affiliate in Minneapolis aired a story about Kelly Bakke of Kix Photography.[1] Kelly had spearheaded an antidrug campaign in a rural Wisconsin town. She took photographs of high-school students showcasing their antidrug activities and assets—things they considered important enough to keep them from using drugs or alcohol. She photographed the young people acting, reading, playing instruments, playing sports, holding skateboards, meditating, spending time with friends, visiting with family, and more. The local elementary school displayed these portraits around the school to encourage younger children to find their antidrug and stay sober. In showcasing the young peoples' individual gifts as potent antidrugs, Bakke was also showcasing how these gifts serve the common good. Paul tells us we have each been given a manifestation of the spirit for the common good. In this small Wisconsin town, the football player, the skater, the oboist, the actor, and the dedicated student now saw their unique manifestations of the spirit as public gifts intended for the common good.

The Call Is Constant

God's call comes packaged in a variety of ways. We might hear it in the lyrics of a song, in the comforting words of a friend, or the challenging words of a teacher. My mother taught me to recognize the song of a cardinal. I began to hear cardinals everywhere! Of course, those cardinals had been singing all along, but I never knew what I was hearing. God's call to a life lived for the common good is a constant drumming on the souls of our young people. It might be more intense and more noticeable at certain times or in certain places. As they learn to notice it, they begin to encounter it regularly. Development for the undeveloped consumer happens in fits and starts, with an individual sometimes lagging behind her peers for months. God's call is constant. The called cocreator is never more or less called than her peers.

When researching how young people talk about God's presence and activity in their lives, it was common to hear them describe their experiences as both wildly new and strangely familiar. I have found this to be true beyond my research project as well. Young people will often explain their mountain-top experiences in similar ways. Whether they have been on a mission trip, wilderness adventure, a week at camp, or a weekend retreat, they will describe their experiences as new and eye-opening yet familiar. Ephesians 2:8–10 says, "For by grace you have been saved through faith, and this is not your own doing; it is the gift of God—not the result of works, so that no one may boast. For we are what he has made us, created in Christ Jesus for good works, which God prepared beforehand to be our way of life." These experiences seem to deepen their awareness of that call, which God had prepared beforehand to be their way of life. It is as if they recognize and know this call deep within their bones.

The Call Is Sometimes, but Not Always, Specific

There are times when this constant drumming of God's call on our souls manifests itself in a specific way. The call, in general, is to partner with God in bringing about life and reconciliation. This general call will, at times, require specific action. Just as there is not a specific pathway or plan with the call, there is not always a specific action required either. Following Christ into the world to love and serve the neighbor can sometimes be ambiguous.

On Ash Wednesday, March 5, 2003, high-school and college students across the country walked out of classes and schools in protest of America's pending invasion of Iraq. Some of the young people in the congregation I was serving heard about this protest and brought it up at the end of our Sunday gathering on March 2. They wondered if they should or should not participate. What followed was a rich conversation about how we as Christians feel about war and whether we support or protest war. Every young person there that evening sensed a call to discover more about how we can or should respond to war as Christians. Not everyone agreed that a walkout was the best form of action. Our young people were experiencing a call, but there was no consensus and they could not identify a single universal action.

> The call, in general, is to partner with God in bringing about life and reconciliation.

The Call Always Requires Discernment

Because the call is ambiguous and not always specific, it will always require discernment. Discerning the call is a process of sifting through a young person's options while considering the context, needs, assets, and opportunities. The call is rarely clear. In fact, it is wise to be wary of those who seem to be too clear about their call.

Our community was wrestling with an appropriate Christian response to the threat of war. Thirty-five young people and seven adults stuck around at church for an extra forty-five minutes to wonder together. Our young people had entered the discernment process, sifting, weighing, and debating their options. Their desire to wonder together about what their faith was calling them to do and be in that moment was deeply moving for me. Their commitment to challenge and affirm one another also moved me. Their commitment to one another was rooted in the spirit of discernment, and not just in decision-making. They were weaving their own desires and fears together with what they believed to be God's desires and fears. They practiced listening to their own stories while considering God's story, and vice versa. Such is the work of discernment.

Discernment Requires Community

Discerning God's call is never a solitary action. It always involves one's community. The call is constant, but often hidden. It is sometimes hidden in the wisdom and words of our community. It is external and not internal. It comes from beyond us. Our calls also do not exist in isolation. Our gifts and calls come to us as members of a community, as members of the body of Christ. Therefore, we need our communities to help us better understand how God might be calling us at any given time.

As the members of our community were discovering their calls in light of the impending war, Thomas stepped into the role of devil's advocate. Thomas was a critically thinking ninth grader. Whenever someone would say they were pretty sure God was calling them to take a particular action, Thomas would chime in and ask, "How do you know it's not the devil asking you to do that?" He would ask this of those who were ready to protest and those in full support of the invasion. Discernment requires this type of community. Not only does the call come from outside the individual, it is also discerned outside the individual. We all have voices within us ready to convince us we are bigger heroes or failures than we are. A community pushes back against these myths and holds us accountable to both our potential and our limits. Discerning our call in community does not assume, or even expect, consensus.

The undeveloped consumer does not hear that she has a call to live out God's mission right now. She is led to believe that she has not yet fully developed and, therefore, she cannot contribute in a meaningful way until she enters adulthood and develops the maturity and expertise needed to be a contributing member of society. If we believe the undeveloped consumer is real, then we are also saying our young people are not fully human. Yet, we know this is not true. We believe God calls and equips our young people as members of the body of Christ. Therefore, we can no longer perpetuate this lie that our young people are undeveloped. They are called. They are in process. They are not the people they will be tomorrow or next year. God calls them into an unfolding life of discovering their gifts and discerning how

God is inviting them to participate with God in God's work. We know in our hearts that our young people are called and not undeveloped. Now it is time to allow that belief to reshape our ministry with them.

Implications for Ministry

As with almost everything, there is no simple, magical way to help a young person clearly hear God's call in her life or accomplish anything else this book proposes. It is best to imagine the implementation of this project's implications for ministry as being similar to how Israel remembers the words of the Shema. The Shema is found in Deuteronomy 6:4–5, "Hear, O Israel: The Lord is our God, the Lord alone. You shall love the Lord your God with all your heart, and with all your soul, and with all your might." The verses immediately following the Shema implore the Israelites to talk about the Shema with their young people when they lie down and when they rise, when they are home and when they are on the road. Remembering the Shema happens always and everywhere. Such is the case with discerning the call and the implications for ministry discussed in the following chapters.

A place to begin is by helping young people think about their calls in response to needs, gifts, passions, power, and community.

A place to begin is by helping young people think about their calls in response to needs, gifts, passions, power, and community. The following five questions will help start the conversation. Find creative ways to work through these questions with your young people. Do this work with them when you are at home and when you are away; when you wake up and when you lie down.

Needs

What is currently happening in the world that breaks your heart? How do you see God's creation (people, animals, the land, etc.) suffering today? Incorporate current events into your ministry with young people. Resist telling them how they should feel about or react to these current events. Ask them to consider where they see suffering or fear among their peers at school. Get the young people of your congregations engaged in the surrounding community. Teach them how to engage the community, how to listen to the community's story, and how to recognize the needs in the community as expressed by those who live in the community. Help them learn to live life in response to their neighbors' needs.

Gifts

What are some things others say you are good at? Help young people discover their gifts. The Gallup Organization's Clifton Youth StrengthsExplorer is a good place to start for younger teens, and the CliftonStrengths for Students is a good place to begin for older teens.[2] Help them see the gifts and strengths they possess that often go unnoticed by our society. Create opportunities for your young people to utilize their gifts in your congregation and community. Pair young people up with older adults who share the same gifts so the older adult can mentor the young person into that gift, and vice versa. Brag about the gifts of your young people in front of your congregation and in front of your larger community whenever you have the chance. Help your young people talk about their gifts as gifts from God given to them for the common good.

Passions

What are some things you are passionate about—things that bring you joy and energy—even if you do not think you are good at them? We all have things we love to do even if we are not good at them. Adult society has forced our young people into thinking they must excel at everything. We can help our young people identify their passions, even if they are not gifted at these passions. Search Institute calls this a young person's "spark."[3] A spark is that thing that brings a young person joy, energy, and power like nothing else in her life. Pay attention to the things your young people love to do. Teach other adults in your congregation to pay attention as well. Help the young people identify their sparks, place adults in their lives who will help nurture these sparks, and create opportunities for your young people to practice their sparks. Help them talk about their passions as gifts from God as well. Consider starting a photography project like the one by Kelly Bakke, described earlier in this chapter. Take photographs of each young person in your congregation posing in a way that demonstrates their spark. Display these prominently in your congregation.

Power

What is your circle of influence? Where do you have power to make the kind of positive impact you wish to see? The optimism of our young people generally leads them to believe they can change the entire world at once. It is important to help them retain optimism while also being realistic. Help the young people in your congregation identify their circle of influence or the places where they have power, authority, and responsibility that will allow them to impact the type of change they wish to see. By helping them know where they do have power, you will also be helping them recognize where they do not have power. Help them unpack why they do not have power in certain places. Help them learn how to engage others' power and assert their own in constructive ways. It is essential that they learn to identify their circles of influence, it is also possible that their circles of influence will expand. Caring adults can play the role of connector, introducing young people to other collaborators and projects that might expand the young person's circle of influence.

Community

What other gifts and assets are in your community that could be helpful as you seek to address that which is breaking your heart?

If a young person is seeking to address an issue that is important to her, and she is lacking the necessary gifts or power, then this becomes an opportunity for her to expand her network of collaborators. Walk through your community with your young people and draw a map of all the resources, gifts, and assets that exist in your community. The Alban Institute offers a free resource called "The Quick and Simple Congregational Asset-Mapping Experience,"[4] which will help you imagine how to do this with your community. Create opportunities for young people to learn about the gifts of other adult members of your congregation. Introduce them to significant leaders in your congregation's community who have power and influence. If you have used StrengthsExplorer with them, then keep referring to their various strengths so they learn to seek out others' strengths and gifts when working to solve a problem.

The rubber really hits the road once we combine these five steps of the discernment process together and help our young people begin to see how they can weave together their gifts, passions, power, and community to address the world's needs that concern them. When we assume our young people are undeveloped, we sell them short and miss out on their gifts and passions. In many states, you must be sixteen years old to drive legally, but you do not need to be sixteen years old to know how to drive a car. You must be old enough to have attended seminary to be a pastor, but God places no age restriction on the ability to preach, pray, prophesy, heal, teach, forgive, or lead. As our young people learn that God has called them, then God will truly begin to do new things that will make our ears tingle.

Discussion Questions

1. Which of the ten points about calling in this chapter (pp. 69–81) do you find most important for your work with young people? Why? Which of the ten theses do you find hardest to believe or accept? Why?

2. Take some time to answer the five discernment questions in the "Implications for Ministry" section (pp. 82–85).

3. What is a creative way you could engage your young people with at least one of these questions?

4. In what ways do you think your congregation's ministry with young people is still dependent upon the assumption that they have not yet developed fully?

5. How does your congregation create and support a community context for young people to discern call and vocation? If you are not doing this, how might you begin?

4

Child of God

For all who are led by the Spirit of God are children of God. For you did not receive a spirit of slavery to fall back into fear, but you have received a spirit of adoption. When we cry, "Abba! Father!" it is that very Spirit bearing witness with our spirit that we are children of God, and if children, then heirs, heirs of God and joint heirs with Christ—if, in fact, we suffer with him so that we may also be glorified with him.

—Romans 8:14–17

I remember my children's baptisms vividly. I tend to be an emotional guy, and I knew I would get choked up. I was able to hold it together until I heard the pastors say their names followed by "child of God, you have been sealed by the Holy Spirit and marked with the cross of Christ forever." I had used this blessing throughout my years in ministry to help families celebrate their children's baptismal anniversaries, as a blessing on our young people before leaving for trips, and at the end of significant experiences. I knew the power embedded in these words—their spirit of adoption—but I did not fully know the power of these words until they were spoken over my own children. To be a child of God is to have an identity that we do not earn or choose but simply receive through the grace of God. This chapter explains the limits and dangers of talking about identity as an achievement and offers *child of God* as a more faithful alternative. Our young people are not identity-less; God identifies them as children of God.

The Crisis of Trying to Achieve Identity

Erik Erikson has made significant contributions to the field of developmental psychology and our understanding of human beings. He introduced the concept of development as a product of the interaction between the self and one's context, or historical moment. Many will say he was one of the first to make the case for an understanding of development across the lifespan, rather than limiting it to childhood. However, like all bold trailblazers, Erikson is not without critique. The fields of youth work and youth ministry have been naïvely dependent upon Erikson's claim that adolescence is a time of life defined by the urgent resolution of one's identity crisis. This assumption, and its misinterpretations, have aided in the proliferation of the undeveloped-consumer myth. The assumption that our young people lack identities fits into the narrative of being undeveloped and that they must consume to achieve an identity. Therefore, it is important to spend a moment explaining why assuming we achieve identity in adolescence actually creates a crisis rather than resolves one.

Erikson claims we develop through eight stages. We each must resolve a different conflict at each stage of our development before being able to move forward in a healthy way. The conflict, or crisis, we must solve during adolescence is that of identity versus role confusion. According to Erikson, this crisis emerges as we begin to experience the physical changes of puberty. These changes lead us to believe we are now different persons than we were as children. We also begin to wonder about other peoples' perceptions of us. The young person successfully achieves or constructs her identity by reconciling these various perceptions. Role confusion happens if the young person cannot reconcile these perceptions and is unable to "settle on an occupational identity which disturbs individual young people. To keep themselves together they temporarily over-identify, to the point of apparent complete loss of identity, with the heroes of cliques and crowds."[1] We seem to assume we must latch on to an identity that is outside ourselves.

Erikson's theory is problematic in a few ways. First, it has been famously critiqued, or nuanced, by Carol Gilligan, who demonstrates how Erikson's theory is one of many developmental theories that normalize the male experience over against the female experience. She says, "[we assume] for men, identity precedes intimacy and generativity in the optimal cycle of human separation and attachment, for women these tasks seem instead to be fused. Intimacy goes along with identity, as the female comes to know herself as she is known, through her relationship with others."[2] She is critiquing Erikson's idea that a young person must know himself before he is able to experience intimacy or agency. Gilligan knows the opposite to be true for young women, who come to know who they are *through* intimacy and agency. We now know this to be true for young men as well.

The second problem is the oversimplification of the teenage years as the time in life when our sense of self is forming. Our sense of self, or identity, is always emerging and evolving, not only as teenagers. New relationships, medical emergencies, losses, achievements, and travel are just some of the things that impact our understanding of ourselves throughout the life span. This leads to the third problem. Erikson offers only a partial description of reality—humans seek identity, assume identity must be achieved or constructed, and experience this intensely during the teenage years. This is one interpretation of what we actually experience. However, we can theologically reimagine this experience in a way that is more hopeful and true to Scripture's witness of God's desire for us. Our young people are not searching for or constructing an identity; God has already identified them! God's divine movement into a

> Our young people are not searching for or constructing an identity; God has already identified them!

relationship with them has already gifted them with their identity as children of God.

Erikson is correct in that we do experience a certain level of identity confusion. However, he is wrong to assume we must resolve this confusion before we can experience intimacy, that it primarily happens during adolescence, and that identity is something we achieve or construct. Youth work and youth ministry have uncritically latched onto Erikson's theory and proclaimed identity confusion as the diagnosis for many problematic behaviors that surface among our young people. Our young people do not act out as an expression of not knowing who they are; they act out as an expression of frustration with an adult-controlled world that fails to see them for who they really are.

Identity as Gift

Identity is a gift, not an achievement. Our young people are not without identity. If our work with them leads them to believe they must achieve or construct an identity for themselves, then we have done them a disservice. Such sentiment does not mean our identities are clear, easily understood, and quickly embraced. It takes time and work to come to terms with one's identity. It is not easy to believe that God has identified you as a child of God. Nor does it mean one's identity is a restrictive, scratchy suit forced upon our young

> When God gifts us with the identity of child of God, it does not close doors or opportunities.

people. God's move to identify us as children of God is not a restrictive move but a liberating move. It functions in the same way we spoke of vocation earlier. When God gifts us with the identity of child of God, it does not close doors or opportunities; rather, it opens doors and possibilities.

The best way to demonstrate how identity is a gift is to explain two differing views of the *imago Dei*, or the belief that God creates us in God's image. The theological claim of *imago Dei* comes from Genesis 1:26–27.

> Then God said, "Let us make humankind in our image, according to our likeness; and let them have dominion over the fish of the sea, and over the birds of the air, and over the cattle, and over all the wild animals of the earth, and over every creeping thing that creeps upon the earth." So God created humankind in his image, in the image of God he created them; male and female he created them.

God's work of creating us in God's image has been explained in two ways: the *substantialist* explanation and the *relational* explanation.[3]

The substantialist explanation claims it is our substance that makes us God-like. Some, though not many, have interpreted this to mean we are in God's image because we share some physical characteristic with God. You can see where this could get out of hand, and it has. This line of thinking has allowed some to claim that men are closer to God's physical image. Others have claimed those with lighter skin are closer to God's physical image. Most scholars reject this interpretation of the substantialist explanation, but there is no denying the powerful impact it has had on Christianity and cultures around the globe.

A more common interpretation of the substantialist explanation focuses on our substance that is less physical and more internal. Some would say it is the soul, or the mind, or the capacity for reason or morality that marks us as in the image of God. This substantialist explanation of the *imago Dei* is problematic for three reasons. First, it easily blurs the line between God and humankind. It leads us to believe the more we embrace the *imago Dei*, the less dependent upon God we become. Second, it can still lead to the dehumanization of certain populations. What does it mean for those who do not possess the mental capacity to reason if we insist our connection with God lies in our ability to reason? Are they not created in God's image? The same is true for any other human attribute we point to as evidence of the *imago Dei*. Third, it promotes human beings to the top of creation, making us closer to God than the rest of creation. This argument lends itself to the justification of humans' mistreatment of creation for our own means. As you can see, the substantialist explanation of the *imago Dei* falls short. There is no physical, spiritual, or cognitive attribute that serves as evidence of the *imago Dei*.

The relational explanation holds great power and promise for our young people. There is nothing we possess that makes us an image of God. Rather, it is God's movement into relationship with us that connects us with God's image. Douglas John Hall says, "To be *imago Dei* does not mean to have something but to be and do something: to image God."[4] It is God's commitment to us, through Christ, that transforms us into the *imago Dei*—those who image God. So it is with identity. It is true, we are in search of identity. It is false to assume identity is somewhere out there waiting for us to discover it or create it. Rather, God gives us our identities as children of God and makes us in God's image in the same movement. A young person might still struggle to grasp and understand his identity as a child of God, but as he comes to understand it, he will see that it is a gift that has been there all along. Our call, which is the calling of the whole body of Christ, is to help our young people become who they already are, children of God.

What Does It Mean to Be a Child of God?

Proclaiming someone to be a child of God is nothing to take lightly. There is power in those words. They mean something. All we need to do is revisit the discussion in chapter 2 on how Jesus exalted children in his time. He saw them not only as inheritors of God's kingdom but also as exemplars of how one lives into God's kingdom. The word *child* does not just denote a certain type of relationship (which it does), it also denotes a certain value-laden position or role. To be claimed as God's child is to become a living example of God's kingdom on earth. Again, there is nothing within us that makes this happen; rather, it is God moving into relationship with us.

We are children of an adopting God. Adoption is good news for those who are troubled by the *child of God* metaphor. Some of us have had very painful experiences as someone's child. Others might not know whose child they are. The word *child* might not always be a comforting word. For those persons, there is hope in the biblical expression of God as an adopting God. Both Moses (Exod 2:10) and Jesus (Matt 1:20–25) are adopted children. Scholars point to the Hebrew prophets, who often use adoption language to speak of God's relationship with Israel. Paul's letters in the New Testament use adoption language when explaining how gentiles can also be part of Christ's church. Adoption is an important way to understand how we become children of God because "it makes clear that membership in God's family is always the result of God's activity . . . [it] transcends the boundaries and barriers set by biological and ethnic identity . . . it can be used both of individuals and of [communities] . . . [and it] reminds us that the identity of faithful people is in the identities God gives us rather than the identities we give ourselves."[5] You are a child of God because God has chosen to identify you and adopt you.

To be a child of God is to be adopted into a universal and timeless family of God. It is to be made a living example of the kingdom of God. Lastly, it is characterized by "infinite openness" to God's future.[6] Just as a child is wide-eyed and open to whatever may come her way, a child of God is wide-eyed and open to God's future blessings and call. This openness of the child is now available to all who are children of God, regardless of age. This openness prevents us from closing ourselves off when we encounter fear or anxiety. This openness is rooted in a hope and trust that God is always working for redemption in our world. Being a child of God means we are open to that which frightens us, open to those who are different from us, open to the impossible ways God's grace shows up in our world. Do you remember the call of Samuel at the beginning of chapter 3? The word of God was rare, and visions were not widespread, but the child Samuel possessed infinite openness. Soon the word of God and the visions returned to God's people. Telling our young people they will not know who they truly are until they search and find an identity does not generate hope in their lives. But incredible hope and possibility abound when they come to realize they are already children of God.

> A child of God is wide-eyed and open to God's future blessings and call.

All of this makes the question of identity sound easier to answer than it really is. We must also look at two things that are important to include in any current conversation about identity—the commodification of identity and diversity. These pressing issues both impact our theological process and are impacted by our theological process. If we do not address these issues with our young people, then we are leaving them to navigate the waters of identity on their own. Commodification and a fear of diversity are two very powerful ways sin wraps itself around our young people, and they both can muddy the waters of identity.

Commodification of Identity

In chapter 1, we reviewed the historical emergence of the adolescent. By the late 1940s, an obvious youth culture had been created through the merging of multiple social changes. This burgeoning youth culture piqued the interest of corporations and marketers. They saw the low-hanging fruit of a niche market waiting to be exploited. *Seventeen* magazine led the charge in 1944 as the first magazine published specifically for teenagers. Its original intent was to take teens seriously and provide a medium through which they could engage the larger world.[7] However, it quickly became primarily a method for advertising products to young people. As youth *culture* became youth *cultures*, the marketing of products became the marketing of identity.

In 2001, *Frontline* produced a documentary called *The Merchants of Cool*, which provided insight into the world of corporate advertising toward teens.[8] It shows us the predatory world of marketing to teens. Companies conduct focus groups and market research to understand this niche market and generate products the young people will purchase. They essentially create a feedback loop. The marketers interview the youth to find out what is "cool," and then they take those ideas back to their corporations and mass produce, package, market, and sell "cool" right back to the youth. This is how we turn young people into commodities. Marketers exploit these self-expressions and then sell them back to young people. The documentary shows us how this feedback loop can go terribly wrong.

> But what lessons do MTV and other companies draw from this exhaustive and expensive study of teenagers' lives? Does it result in a more nuanced portrait of the American teen? In "The Merchants of Cool," FRONT-LINE introduces viewers to the "mook" and the

"midriff"—the stock characters that MTV and others have resorted to in order to hook the teen consumer. The "midriff"—the character pitched at teenage girls—is the highly-sexualized, world-weary sophisticate that increasingly populates television shows such as *Dawson's Creek* and films such as *Cruel Intentions*. Even more appealing to marketers is the "midriff's" male counterpart, the "mook." Characterized mainly by his infantile, boorish behavior, the "mook" is a perpetual adolescent: crude, misogynistic—and very, very angry. But also very lucrative. . . . "What this system does is it closely studies the young, keeps them under constant surveillance to figure out what will push their buttons," says media critic Mark Crispin Miller. "And it blares it back at them relentlessly and everywhere."[9]

This economy depends upon the cultural assumption that one must search for an identity. If our young people believe this external search is necessary, then corporations will continue to market their products as essential components in the identity starter kit. Identity is not for sale; it is a gift. Elizabeth Conde-Frazier articulates the power of this gift in writing about identity among children who are undocumented.

These persons and families refuse to live thinking of themselves only as "illegal aliens" or "undocumented persons." They draw their identity from a higher source, insisting that they are equal to every other human being. They persevere despite the limitations of their context and push back against language and laws that deem them as non-persons or persons unworthy of equal status. They create strategies of survival insisting that their "human status" and the injustices existing in the two countries gives them a right to disrupt the orderly classifications produced by the state. They push us all toward a status of dignity and justice.[10]

This commodification and classification of identity rings loudly in the ears of our young people, and it will take slow and steady work on the part of faith communities to help them hear God telling them they have already been gifted with dignity and justice as children of God.

Identity and Diversity

The church's response to, or engagement with, diversity can also muddy the waters of identity. In the spirit of Christian unity, we can easily begin to whitewash our differences. Verses such as Galatians 3:28—"There is no longer Jew or Greek, there is no longer slave or free, there is no longer male and female; for all of you are one in Christ Jesus"—can make it sound as though becoming a child of God erases all that makes us unique and different from others. The tower of Babel (Gen 11:1–9) is often interpreted as God introducing diversity as punishment for peoples' pride and arrogance. Members of the dominant culture find it easy to embrace this view that God prefers sameness to difference. It is easy for those of us who are white, middle-class, Christian, cisgender, heterosexual, able-bodied men to assume we do not have a distinct culture because we are conditioned to having everything around us reflect our "normalcy" back to us. Our privilege can lead to one of two assumptions. One assumption is that God prefers the dominant culture and all others must assimilate. There is no shortage of horrific examples of this assumption put into practice in the history of Christianity. The second assumption seems benign but is still destructive. If you assume you do not have a culture, then it is easy to assume God is not overly interested in our distinct differences, which is false. It is in our diversity, not our sameness, where we begin to see the beauty of God. "Community is built out of diversity."[11]

Some scholars have pointed out how the miracle of Pentecost seems to bring the punishment from Babel full circle. They claim God's Spirit solves the "problem" of diversity at Pentecost as those present become united in the hearing of the gospel. Eric Barreto, however, has a different point of view. He says,

> Despite their sharing of a faith that draws them from great distances, these gathered masses are not homogenous; they are not all entirely alike. It is this scene of ethnic and linguistic diversity in which the Holy Spirit makes a grand appearance. Each person hears the gospel proclaimed in her own language. The Holy Spirit does not speak with *one* language but with all the languages of the human tableau.[12]

They hear the gospel in their own languages. Diversity, according to Luke-Acts, is not a problem to solve but a blessing through which God reveals Godself. There is no need to see differences as a threat to Christian community. Rather, "prejudice and racism inject our differences with the sinful notion that our difference leads to superiority and inferiority or the distorted belief that our differences are merely cultural cues for determining who is in and who is out, rather than emblems of God's gift of diversity."[13]

The church's inability to speak honestly about the sin of systemic racism also threatens a young person's ability to live into their identity as a child of God. Evelyn Parker found this to be particularly true for African American youth. In her important study on the spiritual lives of African American youth, Parker discovered what she called fractured or fragmented spirituality among young people who were unable to talk about racism as sin. Their spirituality was fragmented in that they expressed personal belief and piety but were unable to imagine an "intricately woven life of divine and human self-understanding that expects God's transformative power and acts in God's transformative power against economic, political, and social domination."[14] Their churches had not helped them see racism as the sin that it is, nor did their churches help them know how to resist it. Parker calls churches to embrace the spirituality of emancipatory hope for African American youth that "is a holistic or integrated spirituality that understands God's salvation even in the midst of racism."[15]

> There is no need to see differences as a threat to Christian community.

As we strive for more inclusive congregations and communities, it is important that we not whitewash our differences in the process. We cannot assume the culture of a congregation is neutral space where everyone can set aside their differences and find common ground. We must be willing to engage differences and allow those differences to change our congregations. We are to help each young person embrace her differences as unique aspects of the person God calls her to be. God does not claim a black young person, a gay young person, a transgender young person, or a young person with cerebral palsy as a child of God so that young person can lay down her uniqueness and be just like everyone else. Being children of God does not make us all the same; it simply makes the children of God reflect God's mosaic. Constructed and achieved identities are easily shed or discarded; being made a child of God does not require us to discard any part of us.

Becoming Who We Already Are

I have spent twenty years in the field of children, youth, and family ministry. In that time, I have encountered many young people who have reaffirmed this understanding of our God-given identity as children of God. I have been with hundreds of young people—children, young teens, older teens, and college-age young adults—when they have discovered their identities as children of God. The stories of two young women, in particular, will enhance some of the points I have made throughout this chapter. I know both well and have asked permission to share their stories and their names. I do this as an expression of my gratitude to them for helping open my eyes to the dangers of assuming identity is our achievement and to the profound hope that comes in knowing identity is a gift from God. It is my claim that our identity as children of God is both new and old. It is something we come to experience as our old sinful selves die and our new lives rise. However, it is also something as old as time. Although we might encounter this call to live as children of God as something new, there is always something strangely old and familiar about it. You will see that tension in these stories.

Sunday Night Me, Monday Morning Me

Erin was a ninth grader when I arrived as the new director of Youth and Family Ministry at her church. She was the middle daughter of a family that was very involved in the church. I knew right away that I was going to enjoy working with Erin. She had a sarcastic wit I appreciated. She was a smart aleck, and in my book, that was a good thing. I was like Erin in that way. I have always liked to push the envelope of sarcasm, humor, and appropriateness. Such behavior comes naturally to me and, unfortunately, has gotten me into trouble on multiple occasions. I imagine this was the case for Erin as well.

Erin grew into a strong leader in our youth ministry. She was someone we could count on to be the first to jump into any experience. We knew she would sign up and be an active participant in whatever was happening. She was outgoing and extroverted. She was also one of our peer ministers, coleading a small group of her peers with an adult from the congregation on Sunday evenings.

I remember when she hit a low point. I did not know exactly what was going on, but I knew she was struggling. She seemed to be distancing herself from some of her friends, especially from one who had been her best friend most of her life. She seemed uncomfortable and shifty, always scanning the room and glaring at people out of the corners of her eyes. It seemed she no longer trusted anyone in our faith community.

Erin and I finally had the opportunity to talk. I am not one to pry, so I let her share only what she was comfortable sharing. She did not share details with me, but she expressed her existential struggle in a simple yet profound way. She said, "I've just come to realize I like the 'Sunday night me,' but not the 'Monday morning me.'" I knew what she meant. I had been there myself. She was proud of the leader she had become in our ministry. Her peers at church looked up to her and appreciated her leadership, and the adults in our community resonated with her as well. People appreciated having her around, sarcasm and all. But her interactions with people outside of our ministry context were less desirable. She was trying to find her niche within the culture of her high school. She had some struggles and setbacks and relied on her sarcasm as a defense mechanism. She burned some bridges along the way. She was longing for consistency in her identity. Theologically, we might say Erin was experiencing the fullness of the *simul justus et peccator*, the theological claim that we are all always simultaneously sinner and justified, and it did not feel good. She wanted to shed the sinner and simply be all (and only) justified.

Erin had a hard time believing these two aspects of her identity could coexist. She was under the assumption that becoming a "good Christian leader" meant every part of your life would get better, making you friendlier, more cooperative, and harder working. This just is not true. We all have moments when we shine and live up to our presumed full potential. But often, we fail to be that person we want to be. Erin's experience was not all that different than the experiences of her peers.

My message to Erin was consistent. God had made her and claimed her. She was a child of God, flaws and all. She did not have to prove she was worthy of anything. Rather, she could live her life learning to accept this gift God had given her. My mantra and ongoing prayer for Erin was, "Become who you already are." Erin was already a fantastic young woman with outstanding gifts of leadership.

> My mantra and ongoing prayer for Erin was, "Become who you already are."

She was God's beloved child on Sunday nights and Monday mornings. Identity is not an elusive holy grail we must hunt for or earn; it is who we already are.

Erin is now in her early thirties. She is a leader in her congregation and recently wrote the following in a note to me,

> It's funny to me that you saw so much in me that I am
> able to see now. I am currently the vice president of our
> church council and I lead the mutual ministry commit-
> tee, serve on the fellowship and stewardship committees,

teach Sunday school, am on the WELCA board, and now lead our newest women's group. A friend and I are currently doing a wonderful Bible study and I hope they will let me lead it during Sunday school hour next fall.[16]

Erin might still struggle to believe God loves her as she truly is. We all share that struggle. But she continues to become who she has always been, a child of God.

I Am Child of God. I Am Woman. I Am Black.

Rozella is a dear friend of mine. She has been a strong leader in the Lutheran church. Now in her mid-thirties, she exercises her leadership as a coach, writer, teacher, preacher, and public theologian. As the owner of RHW Consulting, she helps organizations and individuals come to a deeper understanding of who they are and how they can live into that identity. She is also the director of Mission Houston, a gap-year program for young adults living in intentional community in marginalized neighborhoods and learning to live and practice God's desire for justice. She is a strong woman, and her identity story is lovely.

I tell Rozella's story for two reasons. First, she grew up as a third-generation Lutheran in the Evangelical Lutheran Church in America (ELCA), which is the whitest denomination in America.[17] The ELCA is the context from which I write. Second, Rozella is a young black woman who grew up in this predominantly (96 percent) white denomination. The ELCA is founded upon Martin Luther's theology, which was heavily influenced by the New Testament writings and theology of the apostle Paul.

Therefore, it is no surprise we Lutherans love to quote Galatians 3:28 when confronted with our lack of diversity: "There is no longer Jew or Greek, there is no longer slave or free, there is no longer male and female; for all of you are one in Christ Jesus." As mentioned earlier in this chapter, these are easy words to say when you are a member of the dominant culture. We have mistakenly associated Lutheranism with white Northern European American culture. In turn, we assume that if someone wants to be or become Lutheran, they will adopt this culture rather than the Lutheran theological framework. Our error has been to assume unity through uniformity, though we would never have used those words. Letty Russell warns that "when dominant groups seek community by exclusion and subordination, they end up subverting community because unity and uniformity are a contradiction in terms."[18] Rozella's story of identity is a wake-up call to predominantly white churches first to recognize our congregations should find their source of meaning in theology (confessions about God) and not culture (a potluck menu). And second, that we cannot gloss over the physical and cultural differences of our young people in the spirit of unity. Unity happens not in spite of differences but because of differences. Uniformity eliminates differences. Unity thrives on differences.

Ask Rozella who she is, and she will tell you, "I am a child of God. I am woman. I am black." She speaks of her identity in terms of her physical body and in terms of her character. For her, integration is nonnegotiable. She strives to maintain an integration between her physical being and her character. She is unapologetically black, unashamedly woman, and unrelentingly

Christian. She always begins with her identity as God's beloved child. For Rozella, being a child of God means she knows God has crafted her into the image of God. This leads her to claim her physical self as the essence of her identity.

Rozella has grown up with the storytelling, the music, the food, the community, and the movement of black American culture. She has grown up with the embodied spirituality and worship of the black church. Though she has had mostly positive experiences in her primarily white Christian denomination, she has also come to question whether this church really believes it is a church for her. She has grown up at the intersection of her father's African American blackness and her mother's Afro-Caribbean blackness. These are two distinct ways of being black in America, both of which shaped Rozella's understanding of herself as a black woman and as a Christian. If I only assume Rozella to be black, then I miss the nuances that happen at the intersection of these two different types of American blackness.

Rozella's parents worked hard to ensure she grew up embracing her blackness and her Christianity. Her understanding of what it meant to be a woman emerged over time, especially during her time in seminary. Rozella was married at one time to a pastor. She had held a more traditional understanding of the woman's role in ministry and in the home, but she also saw herself as a woman with gifts to share. She struggled to know how to be herself and, at the same time, fulfill the public role of pastor's wife. She figured it out with help from her church and through critical engagement with Christian theology and the biblical text in her seminary classes. She came to know the importance and power of being a woman.

Rozella sees her identity as a combination of what has always been (the things God has endowed her with) and what is becoming (the reality that she is a cocreator with God). She has struggled through divorce and mental-health issues but has never lost sight of who she is. The struggles have taught her lessons that have helped her refine the way she understands and articulates her identity. Her blackness, her womanness, and her Christianity are the core of who she is. Thankfully, no one has ever asked her to place those aspects of herself aside for the sake of unity. Her community taught her to embrace them as God's endowment, gifts that form who she is as God's child. If we fail to realize the uniqueness of our young people, then we will fail in helping them know who God has already created them to be and to become.

> If we fail to realize the uniqueness of our young people, then we will fail in helping them know who God has already created them to be and to become.

Rozella is quick to express gratitude for how her church helped her come to understand who she is. Yet, at the same time, she sees it pulling away. She says,

I grew up feeling at home in the ELCA. This denomination created a lot of opportunities for me to become clearer about who I am. But lately I have found who I am—a young, black woman—is not the church's target audience. The worship, the language, the leadership development, the places and spaces the church shows up or fails to show up do not communicate to me that this church is for me. It has become harder for me to engage this church, because it does not seem to be committed to engaging me, or people like me.[19]

Yet, she is not bitter. Instead, Rozella is hopeful. She believes the church has what young people need. It will come down to us finding the courage and creativity to embrace the uniqueness and intersectionality of all our young people so they might come to see themselves within the unity, not uniformity, of God's children. So, let me leave you with these words from Rozella.

What would it look like if our communities of faith and communities of practice actually understood their role to be curators of experience, of opportunity, of spaces that tapped into the endowed stuff our young people are created with and simultaneously provided them opportunities to create what still could be for themselves and their communities? What might happen if every congregation committed itself to becoming this space where young people of all types can always come together with others who will help them uncover, discover, recover, and create the piece of themselves for their next season of life?[20]

Implications for Ministry

We must approach identity work with young people gently. The undeveloped consumer is a powerful narrative in our culture and has left our young people quite fragile. As with the previous chapter's implications for ministry around a young person's sense of call, identity work does not happen through programs as much as through the slow and steady work of relationships. Therefore, it is important to equip your entire congregation to rethink their assumptions about young people. It will take the entire congregation to change its culture and create an environment of relationships that embrace and inform who our young people are and who they are becoming. Here are some suggestions for making that happen.

Learn to Talk about Identity as a Gift

When you hear young people asking questions of identity or expressing disappointment with their own behaviors or identities, intervene with the good news of God choosing them and identifying them as a child of God. It is a gift, not an accomplishment. Weave this expression of identity into sermons and rituals during worship. Teach families how to bless one another daily as children of God, reminding one another who they truly are.

Learn to Avoid Talking about Identity as an Achievement or Discovery

This is the necessary B-side to talking about identity as a gift. As you learn to think differently about identity, you will notice others using undeveloped-consumer language when speaking about identity. You will hear it in peoples' language, on the news, in the newspaper, and in your local schools. Gently encourage others to let go of this language. Begin with those who are closest to you and with your young people. They will help you challenge this negative understanding of identity as they hear it used. Challenge yourself to write letters to the editor of your local paper if you see this language in print. Challenge school leaders, community leaders, and elected officials if you hear them using this language. Teach your young people and adult volunteers to do the same.

Help Young People Develop a Critical Eye Toward Advertising and Consumption

First, train your own eye to see how corporations target and commodify young people in their advertising. Viewing *The Merchants of Cool*, mentioned above, will help train your eye. Once you see it, you will notice it everywhere. Then, teach others to notice it as well. Incorporate advertisements (print, video, digital) into your lessons with young people. Ask them to express the thoughts and feelings the advertising provokes. Also help them notice society's culture of consumption. Learn about the amount of waste and recycling your community produces. *Material World: A Global Family Portrait* is a collection of photographs by Peter Menzel that starkly compares families and their entire possessions across the world.[21] Spend some time looking at these photographs with your young people. Ask them to explain why we think we need so many things. Help them notice when the church presents faith as a product to be consumed or when it approaches young people as consumers.

Learn to Use Language That Is Inclusive of Marginalized Identities

Spend some time learning about microaggressions and listening for them in your congregation and among your youth.[22] For example, I often used the term *guys* to refer to all the students in the room. One semester, two of my female students took issue with this. They helped me retrain my use of language so I was no longer referring to everyone as guys. I never thought it really mattered, until they helped me realize that it did. I have also had many students over the years at various stages of understanding their gender identity. You can use words that will either shame them or signal that you are safe person for them to talk with about their identity. The same goes for racial and ethnic minorities as well as young people with disabilities. Language that has become normal to those of us who are a part of the dominant culture can often send the message that we are not affirming of someone's identity, even if it is not our intent to send that message.

Create Opportunities for Young People to Encounter Difference and Diversity as Equals

Service projects and mission trips have become the norm in our line of work. However, they can often reinforce negative social structures and warped understandings of identity. We can easily begin to think "these people" need us to come in and help them. Thankfully, the field of children, youth, and family ministry has become critical of these experiences that exacerbate us-and-them thinking or the white-savior complex. Rather than reinforcing these negative, destructive social structures, these experiences can deconstruct those structures and offer new visions of human community. Create experiences where the young people in your congregation work alongside those who are different in abilities, race, culture, or religion, whether these experiences are in your home community or elsewhere. Work to make these experiences an opportunity for the young people to learn the beauty and necessity of difference and diversity.

> Create experiences where the young people in your congregation work alongside those who are different in abilities, race, culture, or religion.

The narrative of the undeveloped consumer is a powerful one, and the fear of being without an identity is very real among young people. It can trigger anxiety, depression, and self-loathing. The message that God identifies and claims them as children of God is good news. We know it to be true; we do not need to make it true. The hard work is in helping our young people know and trust it is true.

Discussion Questions

1. What are the things competing to define a young person's identity in your community?

2. How have you come to know and understand yourself as a child of God?

3. In what ways do you think your congregation's ministry with young people is still dependent upon the assumption that they are identity-less?

4. How would your congregation's ministry with young people change if you took seriously their identities as children of God?

5. What is one thing your congregation can do right away to begin implementing at least one of the five implications for ministry outlined above (pp. 111–15)?

5

Relational

You do not have to be good.
You do not have to walk on your knees
for a hundred miles through the desert repenting.
You only have to let the soft animal of your body
love what it loves.
Tell me about despair, yours, and I will tell you mine.
Meanwhile the world goes on.
Meanwhile the sun and the clear pebbles of the rain
are moving across the landscapes,
over the prairies and the deep trees,
the mountains and the rivers.
Meanwhile the wild geese, high in the clean blue air,
are heading home again.
Whoever you are, no matter how lonely,
the world offers itself to your imagination,
calls to you like the wild geese, harsh and exciting
over and over announcing your place
in the family of things.[1]

We all know despair and loneliness. Human lives are more connected now than ever before, yet we cannot avoid the overwhelming experience of despair and loneliness. However, in her poem Mary Oliver pushes through these experiences to proclaim another reality. If we listen, we will hear our place in the family of things being announced. We belong. We are connected. As Christians, we confess a belief in a triune God. If the Trinity is at the core of God's being, then at the core of God's being is a relationship. This relational God created us for relationships—to be in relationship with one another, with God, and with the whole of creation. We are destined for relationship, not self-centeredness. God knits us together to one another and all of creation. Our feelings of isolation are real and, at times, pervasive, but we know another reality. We know the reality of relationality and connectedness. It is in this reality that we place our trust. This chapter challenges the stereotype of our young people being self-centered and claims relationality as a more accurate description of their reality.

The Self-Fulfilling Prophecy of Self-Centeredness

"Self-centered" is one of the primary assumptions, or stereotypes, adults make about young people. It is not uncommon to hear parents of teens bemoaning the self-centeredness of their children. Anyone who has ever worked with teens knows they can be self-centered; the same is true for individuals in their twenties, thirties, forties, and beyond. All human beings have the capacity to be incredibly self-centered. Nearly all those same human beings can also act selflessly. The self-centered label we apply to young people has its roots in the study of cognitive development. We have misconstrued an important finding from this field and turned it into a description of their social reality rather than their cognitive reality. It has become a convenient way for adults to shame young people for simply being human.

Jean Piaget conducted groundbreaking research in constructing a theory of cognitive development. He used the term *egocentrism* to describe a person's inability to differentiate effectively between herself and others. However, this is also true beyond the teenage years. We all express egocentrism at every level of cognitive development from infancy through adulthood, but it manifests differently at different times based on one's cognitive abilities. In fact, some research suggests adults only appear to be less egocentric because we know how to mask it.[2] It is also important to note that Piaget is using the word *egocentrism* to describe a cognitive function and not a social function.

David Elkind took Piaget's theory and zoomed in on the teenage years to gain a better understanding of egocentrism during this phase of life. Elkind and other cognitive theorists would argue "the conquest of thought" to be the most urgent project of adolescence.[3] Formal operational thought emerges during the teen years. This is the ability to think about thinking. For the first time in their lives, young people can take another person's perspective, or at least understand that someone else might have a different perspective than their own. This is a new skill and one they have not yet mastered in the teen years. According to Elkind,

Egocentrism emerges because, while the adolescent can now cognize the thoughts of others, he fails to differentiate between the objects toward which the thoughts of others are directed and those which are the focus of his own concern. . . . Accordingly, since he fails to differentiate between what others are thinking about and his own mental preoccupations, he assumes that other people are as obsessed with his behavior and appearance as he is himself. It is this belief that others are preoccupied with his appearance and behavior that constitutes the egocentrism of the adolescent.[4]

Our young people are not egocentric, or self-centered, because they think they are more important than others or because they are unaware of others. In fact, it is exactly the opposite. They have become hyperaware and concerned about others. They have a newfound awareness of their interconnectedness and have not yet completely mastered the ability to cognitively process this reality. Again, egocentrism defines a cognitive function, not a social function.

It is now commonplace to use the term *egocentric* as a description of how one behaves socially. For example, it is used to describe why teens tend to be loud and rowdy when they are with a group of peers in a public place. We assume they only care about themselves and not those around them. We misconstrue Piaget's and Elkind's theories when we use them to describe behavior, because their intent is to explain cognitive processes. Truthfully, our young people are highly relational and are coming into a new understanding of and appreciation for this relational reality. They are very aware of others' needs and opinions while at the same time trying desperately to cognitively grasp how they should exist in what seems to be foreign territory.

When we label their behavior as egocentric, selfish, or self-centered, we shame them for simply being human, for having arrived at this new awareness of the world around them and their place within it. Imagine a fourteen-year-old boy coming home from school, still processing his social interactions from the day. His mother is also coming home from a busy day at work. All she wants is some peace and quiet at home, but her son just wants to tell her stories of what happened at school and on the bus. She asks him to be quiet; he complies for a few minutes only to begin telling the stories again. His mother snaps, "Why are you so selfish? Didn't I just tell you that I need it quiet right now?" He was not trying to be selfish. He was acting normally. In fact, he was trying to connect with his mother. Though he might not have been aware of it, he was also simply processing his social interactions cognitively. We have all been that parent or that adult who makes this type of accusation. If we tell our young people their normal *behavior* is selfish, then they will simply begin to believe that *they* are selfish. Maybe the despair and loneliness Mary Oliver addresses in her poem grows from the shame we experience for feeling selfish. We take a word

> Truthfully, our young people are highly relational and are coming into a new understanding of and appreciation for this relational reality.

meant to describe their cognitive reality and use it to define their social reality. *Egocentrism* is a term that describes the cognitive process involved in understanding their social reality. *Relationality* is the term we should be using to describe this social reality, not self-centeredness.

The Reality of Relationality

To explain how relationality describes our reality, it is necessary to begin with a relational understanding of God. Old Testament scholar Terence Fretheim makes the following three claims about God's relationality and its implications: First, "relationality is basic to the very nature of God."[5] Second, "this relational God freely enters into relationships with the creatures."[6] Third, "this relational God has created a world in which all creatures are interrelated."[7] I will use these three claims to organize the next few sections in an attempt to demonstrate relationality as the normal reality for our young people.

Relationality Is God's Nature

You will find a relationship at the center of God's being. At least, this is what we confess as Christians when we confess our belief in the triune God. The claim that God is relational does not only mean God desires relationships. This is true; God does desire relationships, but God's relational nature exists prior to any relationship. The Christian witness of encountering God in three distinct persons yet one substance is the primary reason we claim

God is relational. Fretheim explains the Old Testament writers described God relationally long before Christian theologians began constructing the doctrine of the Trinity. For example, the divine council in Genesis 1:26, "Let *us* create humankind in *our* likeness."[8] God does not function within the realm of isolation; rather, God functions within the realm of community and relationship. God is not only relational; God is a relationship. Our relational reality stems from our relational God.

God Desires a Relationship with Creation

Scripture is full of stories of this relational God tenaciously entering and maintaining a relationship with God's people. In fact, most metaphors used in the Old Testament to describe God are defined by their relatedness (i.e., "husband-wife; parent-child; teacher-student").[9] The Old Testament writers used these metaphors because they believed God had chosen to enter into relationships of these types with God's people. Scripture is a story of God continually creating opportunities for humanity to be in relationship with God. The first books of the Bible lay out this theme. We see this modeled when God clothes Adam and Eve before removing them from the garden of Eden, creating a future for them. We also see it when God marks Cain with a sign to prevent others from harming him before sending Cain away after Cain kills his brother Abel. God creates a future for Cain. We see it when God hears God's people crying as slaves in Egypt and frees them. We see God's desire to be in relationship with creation in dozens of other stories throughout

Scripture. The biblical narrative tells the story of God persistently moving into relationship with God's people, creating new opportunities for that relationship even when it appears the people have blown their last chance once and for all. We are relational because this relational God has created us in God's image. This relational God is in constant pursuit of us. God's act of drawing us into relationship creates and preserves our relational reality.

> We are relational because this relational God has created us in God's image.

Relationality Is Creation's Nature

As the poem says at the beginning of this chapter, we all have a place in the family of things. Humans are not the only relational things God has created. God creates the entire cosmos for relationship. "Interrelatedness is basic to this community of God's creatures. Each created entity is in symbiotic relationship with every other and in such a way that any act reverberates out and affects the whole, shaking this web with varying degrees of intensity."[10] It is shortsighted to speak only of humans as relational. Human beings are relational because God's cosmos is relational and connected. In this cosmos, it is impossible to *be* self-centered. One might *act* self-centered, but one could never *be* self-centered in this interrelated cosmos. Self-centered, self-absorbed, or egocentric might be apt terms for describing the cognitive function involved in differentiating between oneself and another, but they do not describe one's social reality. Our reality is always only relationality.

Jesus and Relationality

Jesus is the incarnation—the continuation and embodiment—of God's relationality. "In the beginning was the Word, and the Word was with God, and the Word was God. He was in the beginning with God. All things came into being through him, and without him not one thing came into being. . . . And the Word became flesh and lived among us, and we have seen his glory, the glory as of a father's only son, full of grace and truth" (John 1:1–3, 14). Jesus is the Word of God in our midst, in the flesh. Jesus is the embodiment of God's Word. This is the same Word that was with God in the beginning when God's Word called creation into being. At the center of God's being we find a relationship. This Word is part of that relationship. The relational Word becomes flesh in Jesus Christ and enters relationship with creation in a consistent and distinct way. Jesus is an extension, a continuation, and the embodiment of God's creative and relational Word.

Throughout the four gospels, we see and hear Jesus acting on and teaching about this relational reality. His parables promote an understanding of Yahweh that is relational rather than distant. They also teach a way to live out one's faith relationally rather than legalistically. More than once Jesus admonishes the Sadducees and Pharisees for prioritizing the law and ritual over relationships, while elevating those outside Judaism as the exemplars of relationality. He consistently reminds his disciples of the importance of relationships as he encourages Mary to sit with Martha at his feet or when he places a child among them as a model of what it means to be great.

In the beginning, the relational triune God creates and draws creation into relationship with Godself. Jesus's life—his actions and teachings—continue to draw creation into a relationship with God. But let's be clear, it is not our success at imitating Jesus's relationality that makes us relational. It is not about what we do, it is about what Jesus does. Jesus's actions come from who he is. Jesus's life and teachings model and promote relationality because Jesus's being is relational within the triune God. Just as we find our identity as children of God in the context of God's relational move toward us, we also find our identity as relational beings in that same context. We are relational because God enters relationship with us, and in Christ we are set free for that very same relational reality.

In his influential book *Revisiting Relational Youth Ministry*, Andrew Root critiques the popular practice of relational ministry with youth when it becomes a ministry of influence. According to Root, Jesus was not in the business of influencing but in the business of relationships. Relationships are not a means to an end. Rather, they are an end in and of themselves. Root points to Jesus as the relational one who is incarnate, crucified, and resurrected. He reminds us that "Jesus remains in his present person, even today, the incarnate, crucified, and resurrected One. He continues as the one who is incarnate for me, crucified because of me and resurrected despite me, and he is all of this for me."[11] Jesus is always *for me*, and therefore always *for you*. As soon as Jesus is *for me*, he then becomes *for you*. Just as when a community of faith shares Communion in the round. One member receives the bread and wine broken and shed *for her*, but as she turns to commune her neighbor, that bread and wine is now broken and shed *for him*. Christ draws me into relationality. Therefore, he frees me to be *for you*. Because Christ also draws you into relationality, he also frees you to be *for me*. Jesus's incarnation, life, teachings, death, and resurrection draw us into relationship with Christ and, in turn, with one another.

Douglas John Hall expands this idea of Christ making us relational through the *imago Dei* to include all of creation.[12] Christ brings us into relationship with God, with our neighbor, and with the entire created cosmos. We can hear Root's phrase "for you" and Hall's phrase "being-with" as relationship. A human being is always a human being-with, meaning we can only know ourselves as relational beings. My hope is that you are starting to see how this current conversation overlaps with our previous conversations about identity and vocation. Your identity as a child of God means relationality is your state of existence. Hall wants us to see that relationality in three ways—with God, with neighbor, and with the cosmos. In chapter 2, this "three-dimensionality of our being-with" describes how vocation liberates young people—by awakening their dependence upon God, their stewardship of creation, and their responsibility for their neighbor.

Young people frequently return from a pilgrimage with one another—a mission trip, retreat, or week at camp—and talk about how wonderful it was. We might be grateful for their experience, but we also might write it off as a nice mountaintop experience and encourage them to reengage real life in the "valley." But what if their experience on their trip was more real than the way we live our daily lives? I believe it is safe to assume our young people experience the reality of their relationality—with God, neighbor, and creation—while on these trips in ways that are more profound than what they usually experience. They know what it means to be relational in all three of these dimensions, and they can feel it reverberating inside them when it is happening. This does not happen to egocentric, self-centered, self-absorbed people. It happens to relational people.

Who You Calling *Self-Centered*?

We do not need to look far to find examples of our young people living into this relationality and shattering this stereotype of self-centeredness. If you have been around teenagers, then I am sure you have seen just how invested they are in relationships, whether friends or strangers. Sometimes their actions are long-term and extremely heroic. Sometimes they are brief and mundane. Either way, it quickly becomes obvious that the term *self-centered* does not come close to defining who our young people are.

Friends Over Wounds

A pit bull attacked my son, Elijah. He and my daughter, Naamah, were playing with their neighborhood friends Carter,

Michele, and Sam. Elijah is fourteen, significantly older than the others. They look up to him like a big brother, and he takes it in stride. It was time for dinner, so they were all heading home. Carter forgot his water bottle, so Elijah ran it back over to his house. When Carter opened the door, his family's pit bull shot out the door and chased after Elijah. Luckily the dog was on a leash, and Carter's grandmother was able to pull it off Elijah, but only after it had bitten Elijah's leg, leaving significant puncture wounds on his calf and shin. He pulled himself together as best he could and walked home. Michele and Sam were still hanging around with Naamah. Elijah calmly asked them to go home and told Naamah to come inside with him. That is when he told her what had happened. He did not want Michele and Sam to know because he did not want them to be scared.

As my wife was cleaning Elijah's wounds, Naamah passed out and hit her head on the floor. It was traumatic for all of us. Elijah, of course, was crying a lot. As he was calming down, I asked him if he was crying because he was still in pain. He said no, he was worried Naamah was hurt, he was worried Michele and Sam were scared, and he was worried Carter would lose his dog.

Everyone turned out to be okay. In hindsight, Elijah's reaction surprised my wife and me. This scary dog attacked him, but he maintained his composure in front of the little kids. He was less concerned about his wounds and more concerned about his sister, the neighbor kids, and the dog. This whole thing happened in just five minutes, but it will forever stand out to me as an example of the kind of person my son is—brave, conscientious, and compassionate. In this moment he was anything but self-centered. This is just one example that disproves the self-centered stereotype of young people. This fourteen-year-old had more concern for his sister, his friends, and a dog than he had for his own leg. That's what it means to be aware of your relationality.

Siblings over Success

Geoffrey was eighteen years old when he waltzed into my classroom with a huge smile across his face and a sparkle in his eyes on the first day of fall semester. He walked right up to me, extended his right hand, and introduced himself. I could tell this young college freshman was charismatic and eager. Ten years later, he is still the only student I have had greet me in that way on the first day of class. Ten years later, I also consider him a friend.

Geoffrey turned out to be a great student. He was majoring in psychology and knew he wanted to enter a profession that would allow him to help people, particularly young people. He was an active leader in his congregation and in other local and national youth programs. I began twisting his arm, encouraging him to consider switching his major to Youth and Family Ministry. We stayed in touch during spring semester. Every now and then we would meet to discuss switching his major. But then I stopped seeing and hearing from Geoffrey. I was concerned. Geoffrey's father had died tragically from an allergic reaction to a shellfish hors d'oeuvre he had eaten at a banquet. The banquet was in his honor, and he did not know there was shellfish in his food. Understandably, Geoffrey had stopped attending classes. He was in mourning. His dad had just died. His mother had died from cancer when he was eleven years old. He was now the only adult responsible for three younger sisters.

At this moment, Geoffrey found himself faced with two options. He could either shrug off this new responsibility to achieve his dreams, or he could step up and keep his family together. In hindsight, he says the decision was a no-brainer. Of course he was going to step up and raise his sisters. He found a part-time job. Extended family helped with meals and finances for a few months, but then they were on their own. Geoffrey and his sisters remained in the family home. They struggled financially. They struggled to function as a family. They had to learn to operate in this new family system amid great sorrow and stress, and Geoffrey was still in his teens. The lives of these four teens became defined by daily sacrifices, daily compromises, and daily sorrow.

Geoffrey's friends still tell him how impressed they were with his decision and how heroic he has been. Geoffrey doesn't see it this way. In his mind, he was doing what anyone else would have done. He does not regret his decision for a minute, but he is aware of what he gave up. It hit him square between the eyes about six months after his father's death. He received a message from friends wondering if he was going to an event on campus they were planning to attend. He wanted to be there with his friends but needed to be at home for his sisters that particular evening. This was when he realized he would have to sacrifice the normal social life of a college student if he and his sisters were going to make life work as a family.

The four siblings made it work. They have all graduated college and are achieving their dreams slowly but surely. Their relationships weathered the storm, and they still care deeply for one another. They all sacrificed for one another over the years but pulled it off. Geoffrey was a teenager who chose to put his own life and dreams on hold so he could raise his sisters. Geoffrey is an exceptional man, both then and now. But I do not think Geoffrey is the exception. I believe many other young people, if faced with the same situation, would make the same decision and sacrifice Geoffrey made. It is impossible to know this young man, to know this story, to know other young people like Geoffrey, and assume they are self-centered. They are fully relational. They know it. When put to the test, their own understanding of their relationality becomes clear. Geoffrey is living proof.

Implications for Ministry

We all carry the knowledge that God has made us for relationships deep in our bones. However, it is not that easy to trust or live into this relational nature. We often feel lonely and isolated, disconnected from other people and from the air, sky, water, forests, and meadows around us. We dive into social media with the hope it will be a social experience. Often it is not, only exacerbating our sense of loneliness and isolation. There are very few spaces left in society where people can gather to do the intentional relational work necessary to be fully human. Our congregations can offer opportunities for our young people to fully understand themselves as relational and not self-centered. They will show us the way, if we let them. Give the following strategies a try.

Develop Relationships

If you want the young people in your congregation to truly understand themselves relationally, then you and your leadership team will need to invest in the hard work of developing relationships with the youth in your congregation and neighborhood. Too often our congregations assume relationships will happen naturally. If relationships are a priority for your ministry, then every time you gather there will need to be intentional work done to initiate and deepen relationships between those who have gathered. Work at the art of developing relationships as opposed to simply hosting events. I recommend the work Search Institute has done on developmental relationships and encourage you to learn from their research and their resources.[13] They explain the nature of positive relationships and offer some practical ideas on how to create, develop, and sustain these relationships in your community.

> Work at the art of developing relationships as opposed to simply hosting events.

Retrain Your Community

It may also be necessary to retrain your community to see and hear your young people as relational and not self-centered. It is paramount that our congregations learn to understand young people in this way, or they will continue to feel judged and shamed in our communities. This does not mean we ignore poor behavior, but it means we understand the source of that behavior to be relationality rather than selfishness. We tend to scold and shame what we imagine as selfish behavior. If we see a behavior as rooted in relationality, then we might receive that young person relationally rather than shun her shamefully. Helping your congregation understand young people in this way will bear much fruit.

Connect All Young People Relationally to the Congregation

It is primarily the responsibility of adults to engage in relationships with young people. But you cannot accomplish this effectively with just a few adults. Work to connect every young person in the congregation to as many adults as possible. It was always my goal to connect every young person to at least five adults in our congregation in a meaningful way. Church staff members—pastors, youth ministers, and so on—come and go. But most congregational members stay for a long time. It is shortsighted to expect the church staff or key leaders to be the only ones engaging the young people relationally. It is the responsibility of the entire congregation. Relationships do not always happen naturally. They take work, and you will need to equip those whom you are asking to do this work.

Support and Strengthen Intergenerational Relationships

Peer relationships are extremely important during the teen years, but so are relationships with parents, other adults, and younger children. Your relational ministry with young people will need to take seriously all these relationships. Again, this only happens if we intentionally work at it. Congregations can creatively enhance and support these relationships through worship, education, and service experiences. There is no shortage of excellent resources designed to help you develop intergenerational experiences and relationships in your congregation. A congregation's ministry with its young people cannot only be peer-based; it must include opportunities to strengthen all other relationships as well. For everything your congregation does with young people, imagine how to do it intergenerationally.

Help Young People Interpret Their Experiences and Emotions Relationally

Last, but not least, it is important that we help our young people come to understand their reality relationally. The more they hear others say they are selfish, the more likely they are to believe it. We cannot let that happen. When you are helping young people process their experiences individually or as a group, be sure to ask them questions that help them think about the experiences relationally. For example, how did this experience help you understand someone in new ways? How did this experience strengthen your relationships? How did it challenge your relationships? When they are processing emotions, help them think through those relationally as well. I remember my son being very upset in sixth grade because his best friend had a girlfriend. Our initial reaction was that he was experiencing jealousy or anger that he did not have a girlfriend. That was not the case; he was experiencing fear and anxiety that he would lose his best friend. We were expecting a selfish reaction to his friends' girlfriend, but his reaction was actually relational. Our young people will benefit from us helping them sort out those emotions. Remember, egocentrism describes a cognitive function—the emerging ability to hold differing perspectives together. It is a cognitive function they need help learning to operate.

We are relational by nature. We do not need to be good at it, as Mary Oliver says in the poem above; we only need to be human. We need only share our despair. Despair opens the door for relationships to pour in. Roberto Goizueta reminds us that "solidarity in the midst of suffering is what reveals to us the ultimate powerlessness of suffering: our common life, manifested in our relationships of solidarity, overcomes all attempts to destroy that life. Suffering shared is suffering already in retreat."[14] Our vulnerability will be met with the vulnerability of others—strangers, friends, family, mountains, rivers, and wild geese. Watch our young people, and you will see them move through our world in an entirely relational way. They could not be further from selfishness if they tried. They know how to live in this world God has created.

Discussion Questions

1. Share times when you have experienced a young person being self-centered. How might this have been an expression of their relationality rather than self-centeredness?

2. Describe some ways you have seen young people demonstrate how relational and selfless they are.

3. How do you think your congregation's ministry with young people is still dependent upon the assumption that they are self-centered?

4. How would your congregation's ministry with young people change if you took seriously their relationality versus self-centeredness?

5. What is one thing your congregation can do right away to begin implementing at least one of the implications for ministry listed above (pp. 132–37)?

6

Created Cocreator

in the dream every word
is red paint
i speak, it look like a murder scene.
they try shutting my lips
with caution tape
but I am burnin' my mouth down.
It's gon' come back to me
a new thing
no troll bridged tongue
no yawping
soundless empty.
in the dream
i am waiting for my mouth to be born
when she is . . .
everything gon' be loud.[1]

In chapter 4, we discussed the dangers of telling our young people they must search for or construct an identity. This false assumption becomes even more dangerous in the context of rampant capitalism. Chapter 4 addressed the challenge to our young peoples' identities. This current chapter takes on the challenge to their agency or power, which rampant capitalism also threatens. In this context, young people quickly realize they either (1) have no agency, or (2) can only exercise their agency in the marketplace as commodified consumers. The commodified consumer might be descriptive of how our young people live their lives and exercise their agency, but it is a path to nowhere. Rather, they should come to know a sense of agency as created cocreators who God draws into relationship, Christ frees for relationship, and the Holy Spirit empowers for the work of restoring creation. As in the poem above, they are waiting for their mouths to be born, and when they are everything will be loud.

Young People as Commodified Consumers

Our society has a way of shutting the lips of our young people with the caution tape of consumption. It is not enough to simply say our young people live in a consumer culture and have, therefore, become consumers. If we are truthful, we also must reckon with the fact our consumer culture has dehumanized our young people and turned them into commodities. Our culture trains them not only to exercise their agency through consumption but also to see themselves as commodities that can be consumed. This, I would say, is the primary way our young people experience bondage in their lives. Consumerism is such a normalized life style; most are not aware of how it has enveloped them and stripped them of the power God's Spirit has given them. This will be a painful section to read, but it is important that our eyes be open.

The Nonagency of Consumers

Those who research youth culture often disagree on whether youth consumption practices are benign or malignant. Those who see it as benign, or harmless, see it as a simple reality of the society we live in. Those who see it as malignant claim consumer culture to be inherently unhealthy and evil. Those who are optimistic in their assessment of youth consumerism see it as a way for young people to exercise their agency through creative expression of identity. Those who are pessimistic— and I fall into this camp—believe it is problematic to equate consumption with agency, particularly today when it is very difficult to exercise one's rights as a consumer. The market simply does not think of its interaction with young people as a way of increasing their agency; rather, the market sees this interaction only as a transaction involving assets who spend and seek to fulfill needs through products.

> The market sees this interaction only as a transaction involving assets who spend and seek to fulfill needs through products.

The field of marketing identifies materialism as an "emerging value" among young people ages nine to fourteen.[2] Stay with that thought for a moment—materialism is an *emerging value*. In fact, this same study constructed a research instrument called the Youth Materialism Scale that measures the materialism of young people to predict who will be better and more loyal consumers. Although they found no relationship between a young person's materialism and their level of happiness, they did find that more materialistic young people shopped more, saved less, liked school less, and performed worse in school.[3] Large sums of money are being spent to learn how our young people consume, why they consume, and how they can become more loyal and reliable consumers. The alternative is not in developing alternative products for them to consume (ministry programs, Christian music, Christian t-shirts, etc.) but in teaching them to resist the narrative that tells them materialism is a value.

Marketers are not interested in agency; rather, they are committed to "consumer socialization." Consumer socialization is a "process by which young people acquire skills, knowledge, and attitudes relevant to their functioning as consumers in the marketplace."[4] This process of socialization is a developmental process that moves through three stages from preschool through adolescence.[5] Descriptions of these stages are not important to this current project. In all honesty, they are not that interesting. However, it is important to see how the fields of marketing and advertising think of our young people developmentally and use science to develop as much product loyalty among our young people as possible. The goal of capitalism is not to promote human development but to use the science of human development to reap more profit. It is also important to note that some of this literature takes a hostile tone toward societal attempts to protect children from these predatory marketing practices. When discussing the marketing of alcohol, tobacco, and illegal drugs, Deborah Roedder John claims "government agencies and consumer groups have had an uneven history of aggressively pursuing consumer protection for children and adolescents in these areas, but the current climate suggests that concerns and research in this area are not likely to abate anytime in the near future."[6] Here you can see how capitalism views as aggressive society's efforts to organize and protect those who are most vulnerable. Henry Giroux accurately diagnoses this new reality when he says youth are "no longer seen as a social investment or the central element of an increasingly embattled social contract, [they] are now viewed as either consumers . . . or as troubling, reckless, and dangerous persons."[7] The market's goal is to convince our young people they are consumers and that materialism is the best way to exercise their agency. Although I am concerned with the practice of consuming, I am most concerned with the identity of consumer and commodity.

> The market's goal is to convince our young people they are consumers and that materialism is the best way to exercise their agency.

The Dehumanizing Effect of Commodification

Benjamin Barber points out that our young people have not only become primarily consumers, but we have also turned them into commodities. He says, "The boundary separating [a young person] from what she buys vanishes: she ceases to buy goods as instruments of other ends and instead becomes the goods she buys."[8] I mention this phenomenon in chapter 4 as the marketing industry's feedback loop. Marketers go in search of "cool," harvesting fashion and music from youth culture and then mass producing it and selling it back to young people. The self-expressions of our young people, or the young people themselves, become the commodity. The market takes this commodity, spit-shines it, and then sells it back to our young people, who consume it until it becomes uncool. "Marketers are scrutinizing virtually every activity kids now engage in . . . and virtually every aspect of their lives. . . . They are influential in actually producing children, that is in raising, educating, forming and shaping them. And they do this in a commodified form; that is, they produce children in order to sell them back to their clients."[9] And this has only become easier and more effective with the emergence of online analytics that make sure we only see news articles and advertisements online that match our interests.

We also see our young people commodified in society's addiction to youthfulness. This book has spent much ink challenging certain dehumanizing stereotypes of young people, but the truth is that adult culture also idolizes youthfulness. Our culture's definition of beauty is not a middle-aged person but a young person. Our marketing practices simultaneously pressure young people to become adults too quickly and pressure adults to make themselves look young forever. Research has revealed "young adults were 65% more likely to view sexually dressed models and 128% more likely to see sexual behavior in ads than mature adults were."[10] Our young people's bodies are sexualized and commodified in print and in real life. In 2016, there were 66,520 identified victims of human trafficking. There were 14,877 traffickers prosecuted and only 9,071 convictions.[11] It is important that we realize commodification of our young people is not only a reality in advertising. Real young people go missing every year as they are stolen and sold to serve as sex slaves, laborers, or soldiers.

The Pedagogy of Commodification

Henry Giroux calls this troubling trend the "pedagogy of commodification."[12] His language is intentional and important to define. A pedagogy is a method of teaching or training. By using this word, Giroux claims there is intentionality behind what is going on. We are not experiencing an accidental symptom of capitalism; we are experiencing its intentional methodology. This methodology uses science and research to be as efficient and successful as possible. This pedagogy of commodification is built upon "an unqualified belief in childhood agency as a mix of self-promotion and consumption and a willingness to render disposable those young people who cannot fulfill the mandate of acceptable consumer habits."[13] It is quite simple to see how social media has only enhanced the need for and means of self-promotion. In the process, it has also enhanced the gap between those who can and cannot participate in this pedagogy.

Those who are not commodified consumers because they are poor or countercultural are deemed unworthy and disposable within this framework. You see this in the practices of gentrification when urban, minoritized neighborhoods are transformed to appeal to wealthy young white people wanting to live in the city. The residents who lived in the neighborhood before its gentrification are considered disposable; the urban development does not take their needs into consideration. New housing and new businesses come into the neighborhood and do not meet the original residents' needs or budget. Roberto Goizueta points out the irony, "the same society which idolizes 'youth' as an ideal tolerates and perpetuates the ongoing destruction of its concrete, flesh-and-blood youths. Gleaming, modern, technologically sophisticated health spas exist side by side with dilapidated public schools and parks; obsessed with 'youthfulness' we ignore our youths."[14] You also see this practice in environmental racism when industry proven to be harsh on the land and its residents is strategically developed in a neighborhood whose residents are mostly minoritized people. This happens with oil pipelines, power plants, transfer stations, garbage dumps, processing plants, and so forth. We have also seen this in the uptick of young black men being killed by police and the dominant society's unwillingness to support the Black Lives Matter movement. White dominant society must ask itself if it believes black lives matter or if it believes they are ultimately disposable.

Our churches are not off the hook. If we believe no one is disposable, and I hope we do, then we must rise to the occasion and challenge this pedagogy of commodification, consumption, and disposability. Our churches can counteract marketing's use of the commodified consumer that teaches young people that their agency it tied to using money to purchase material goods and to promoting themselves as commodities. Instead of cutting young people off from their true agency, we must help them see their identity, their relationality, and their sense of call. We must teach them that their agency comes from being created cocreators.

The Liberated Created Cocreator

The image of the created cocreator flies in the face of both rampant capitalism and the commodified consumer. The created cocreator refuses to believe the best way to express her power and voice is through consumption. She refuses to allow others to turn her into a commodity for others to consume. She also refuses to be written off as disposable or rendered voiceless by a society that sees her as a "thing" rather than the active and creative person she really is. As Christ's church, we are called to give voice to our young people so when they speak and act, they can be heard and seen. We want them to know they can make holy noise. They cannot be commodified because they are God's creation. They will not be defined by consumption because their calling is to cocreate. Oh, how I wish we could help all our young people know this.

The Agency of Creators

The *created cocreator* is a phrase coined by Philip Hefner, professor emeritus of systematic theology at the Lutheran School of Theology at Chicago. It is Hefner's way of describing the human's place within an evolving cosmos created and sustained by God. It has become an extremely popular formula for describing the human being theologically.[15] In order to explain how the created cocreator liberates our young people from the commodified consumer, I will need to deal with each word in this phrase in a somewhat backward manner. But first, a definition of the created cocreator from Hefner himself.

> Human beings are God's created co-creators whose purpose is to be the agency, acting in freedom, to birth the future that is most wholesome for the nature that has birthed us—the nature that is not only our own genetic heritage, but also the entire human community and the evolutionary and ecological reality in which and to which we belong. Exercising this agency is said to be God's will for humans.[16]

Our agency emerges from our relationship with God just as our identity emerges from that relationship. Our agency is God's creative will. Humans have agency because God gifts human beings with the ability to act. It is in the matrix of this relationship and this agency where we participate in the creation and unfolding of both the ecology and culture of God's world. In writing about the spirituality of young adolescent girls amid a toxic culture, Evelyn Parker uses the analogy of dancing to express the way young women assert their God-given agency. She says it is a

> fitting image for a wholesome spirituality . . . amid the toxic social terrain of racism, sexism, classism, and heterosexism in North American society. . . . Dancing signifies a spirituality that offers a liberative hope to adolescent girls, a spirituality through which they view themselves as agents of God dismantling the systems and powers of injustice, moved by the conviction that God is with them in spirit as they act.[17]

Our young people are dancers. They are creative forces in our world. To be human means to have agency. We enact our agency through the work of creating, not consuming. God does not consume the world but draws the world into relationship with God. It is an ongoing creative work. "Yet, we are also creators, using our cultural freedom and power to alter the course of historical events and perhaps even evolutionary events."[18] To consume is to kill. To create is to give life.

Humans have agency because God gifts human beings with the ability to act.

The Humanizing Effect of Creation

Hefner's created cocreator avoids promotion to God's equal simply by being created. Hefner calls this the "conflicted creature," in that the word "created" qualifies the word "cocreator."[19] We

149

are only cocreators because we have been, and are being, created. Being a cocreator does not make us God's equal, we are still created. It is the paradox of this reality that helps us understand what it means to be human.[20] Hefner understands the act of being created as a process, not a one-time event. It is not that we were created, but that we are always being created. Rampant capitalism's commodification of our young people removes their humanity. It turns them into static, consumable things with no agency. The commodified consumer cannot become anything new. On the other hand, being one who is being created provides the possibility of being truly human by always becoming new. The human being is a dynamic, changing, evolving being living within a dynamic, changing, evolving world in a way that impacts the dynamism, change, and evolution of both the human and the world. That is what it means to be created and to be a cocreator. The silly notion that we can enact our agency through consumption cannot even shake a stick at this understanding of power and agency. To be commodified dehumanizes us and turns us into static objects. But recognizing that we are God's created ones humanizes us because it draws us into a dynamic relationship where power is shared. Which of those two options do you think would be more liberating and empowering for our young people?

The Pedagogy of Co-

The antidote to rampant capitalism's pedagogy of commodification is God's pedagogy of *co-*. The *co-* of the created cocreator says something about the Creator and the created. "It implies not simply that we are creating in and of our own right but that our creative acts are in cooperation with God's creative acts in a way that suggests partnership rather than subordination. . . . [It also] implies a God who radically values freedom over control."[21] Our God is a God who shares power. This is counterintuitive to the way our world thinks about both power and God. We do not usually think about power, authority, control as things to share. We also do not usually think about God as one to share God's creative and redemptive power with us. But that is exactly the kind of God we confess. We see this right away in Genesis 1:28 when God commands Adam and Eve to "be fruitful and multiply." God is setting them free to create.

In Dan Erlander's creative interpretation of the biblical narrative, *Manna and Mercy*, he uses the term *wilderness school* to describe the forty years the Hebrew people spent in the wilderness between their exodus from Egypt and their entrance into the land of Canaan.[22] He claims God used this time to reprogram God's people. Egypt had forcefully

> God's world is a world where power is shared.

shaped God's people into commodities and built itself up upon the backs of those who were most vulnerable. God's vision for God's world is very different. God's world is a world where power is shared. Therefore, the Hebrews required a reboot to live into God's vision. In the wilderness, they begin living into God's pedagogy of *co-*.

God's people continually struggle to embrace the pedagogy of *co-* throughout Scripture. They are never fully able to embrace a vision of God as a God who shares power, nor are they ever able to fully embrace a vision of themselves as people who share power. Anyone who has eyes to see and ears to hear knows we still struggle to embrace this pedagogy of *co-* today. We find the image of a God who shares power to be threatening, and we refuse to share whatever power we think we might have. We have come to think of power, agency, and maybe even God as commodities to hoard and consume. The pedagogy of commodification forces our young people into a zero-sum game in which everything, including agency, seems to be a limited resource. We hoard and are fearful of sharing, making it hard to imagine a God who would share. The pedagogy of *co-* draws our young people into God's abundance where they discover power and authority within cooperation and cocreating.

It is difficult to live into this life of the created cocreator. It requires high levels of trust and comes with high levels of responsibility. Life as a commodified consumer is probably easier and more comfortable. Our inability or unwillingness to embrace this life can be thought of as sin. Hefner tells us, "Our sin is both our understandable unwillingness to accept our status as co-creator—even our fear of that status—and our faulty execution of our co-creaturehood, once we are forced to accept it. This sin is both original and actual."[23] For centuries, Christian theology has talked about the human being living in bondage to sin. Now we can see what that looks like for our young people in today's rampant capitalism. To live in bondage to sin means to fear and refuse our status as created cocreators or our faulty execution of it. This bondage can be called the commodified consumer. Jesus Christ is our liberator from this bondage, and our liberated selves are cocreators.

Everywhere I'm Cocreatin'

It is true that we live in the tension between both the commodified consumer and the created cocreator. It is another way to describe life as one who is *simul iustus et peccator*, simultaneously sinner and justified. The struggle is real. The pedagogy of commodification's siren song is alluring, and humans have a tendency to seek the path of least resistance. Yet, there are many examples of young people shedding the old, dead skin of the commodified consumer and living into their lives as created cocreators. Read *I Am Malala* by Malala Yousafzai or *Do Hard Things: A Teenage Rebellion Against Low Expectations* by Brett and Alex Harris and you will witness three created cocreators in action. We all have stories of young people we know stepping up, becoming who they have always been, and embracing their agency as created cocreators. Here are two of my favorite examples.

Safe Cats, Safe Kids, Safe Park

In August of 2012 someone gruesomely burned and staked a cat to a tree in a South Minneapolis park next to an Obama/Biden lawn sign. The local news agencies covered the story as the security threat that it was. FBI agents investigated to determine if the president was in danger. But there was another part to this story most news outlets missed. Luckily, the Twin Cities Daily Planet picked it up.[24] The Twin Cities Daily Planet is small, local, online news source produced by marginalized voices. It is their coverage of this horrific event I want to share with you.

In the wake of this event, one young created cocreator named Spencer sought to bring some peace to the community and some closure around this tragedy. He worked with his parents to create a vigil in the park for the cat and for the park. He and about fifty of his neighbors (half of them were kids) gathered to cleanse the park. They decorated the sidewalk that surrounded the park with chalk drawings of cats and poems about why they love cats and why they love their park. "Some drew their own cats, and some drew original cats. There was a cat angel and a cat guardian with the warning 'We're watching our park.' Near the chalk drawings is a colorful handmade banner proclaiming 'SAFE CATS, SAFE KIDS, SAFE PARK.'"[25] The event included a message from the neighborhood's city-council member, a blessing from a member of the neighborhood's faith forum, homemade cookies decorated with "Safe Cats," a parade around the park, and balloon kittens. We can write this off as a cute story, or we can see it for what it is: a story of a young boy expressing his sense of power and agency as a created cocreator called and empowered by God "to birth the future that is most wholesome for the nature that has birthed us."[26]

Creating New Creations

In chapter 3, we discussed Search Institute's research on sparks when discussing ways to help young people discern vocation. The most frequently identified sparks by young people fell into the category of the creative arts.[27] Yet, the arts are often the first thing cut from our schools when they struggle to make budget. When we cut the arts, we systemically eliminate a primary outlet for our young people to practice being cocreators. This is a perfect example of how our thinking about our young people is shaped by patterns of consumption rather than patterns of creation.

Jordan, Dylan, and Robert all grew up in Hickory, North Carolina. Hickory is a college town with an active theater scene but no venue for showcasing locally written and produced plays. Plus, the state government had drastically cut funding for the arts in North Carolina. These three friends care deeply about the arts in their community and felt called to address this issue. So, one evening in April 2016, these three nineteen-year-olds met in an online video chat to scheme and dream. Their goal was clear—create a way to provide space for original creative works and provide financial support for arts throughout the community.

Just as the Spirit of God hovered over the waters of the formless void at the beginning of creation, this team of cocreators hovered together over their own call and dream. They created the Hickory Playground, "a not-for-profit theater company founded to encourage the creation of new art in the greater Hickory area, while donating proceeds to the arts in public education."[28] Although they found themselves with a compelling vision and the courage to proceed, they really did not have a clue what to do. They were familiar with the area and with the theater world but had no idea how to ask for money, rent a venue, convince local artists to participate, or sell tickets. They did not wait until they had developed these skills. They dove in and simply learned by doing. They sought out mentors. They made mistakes and learned from them. They put in the time and work to create the Hickory Playground, but they also were learning how to be a team.

Their creation has thrived. In 2016, they put together their first event. They partnered local actors with local playwrights and gave these creative teams forty-eight hours to write and rehearse an original one-act play they would perform. It was so successful they "were able to give away $6,000, half to St. Stephen's High School's art department, and half to Hickory High School's art department. That financial support allowed those two schools to greatly increase their budget for the 2016–2017 academic year, which in turn allowed their students to more fully experience everything the arts can offer." Their second annual event, in 2017, was even more successful, producing "8 original plays, along with several special performances [and surpassing their] $10,000 goal. . . . The Hickory Playground plans on donating $8,000 back to the arts in public schools and community projects."[29]

Jordan, Dylan, and Robert were not going to wait around for the government, the church, or any other organization to finally invest in this work. They knew they could do it. The popular term for this type of work today is "innovation." These three friends were innovative because they are cocreators. Innovation happens when cocreators take vocation seriously and recognize the opportunity at hand as their gifts, passions, and influence merge with their neighbors' needs. Young people are not undeveloped, identity-less, self-centered individuals running around like parasites looking for the next product to consume. They are creative spirits, cocreators, with great things to offer our communities. The Hickory Playground is a creation that creates community for the sake of ongoing creation. It is a gift that keeps on giving, and it is a creation that keeps on creating. And teenagers started it.

It's easy to see just how creative and collaborative our young people are. Their creative and collaborative spirits come from a creative God who has called them into the work of cocreating "the future that is most wholesome for the nature that has birthed us."[30] Spencer, Jordan, Dylan, and Robert do not all believe in God. They are not all practicing Christians. They are not all religious. Yet, they are all seeking to birth the most wholesome future for their communities and, in turn, our world. And we get to be midwives. In the words of the poem at the beginning of this chapter: they are waiting for their mouths to be born, and when they are everything will be loud. And . . . our ears will tingle.

Implications for Ministry

If you and your congregation have been working through the implications from the previous chapters, then chances are you will already be well on your way toward addressing this issue of cocreator versus commodified consumer. But there is always more work we can do. Again, I offer the following ways you can put this work into practice immediately. It is most important that you also do the hard work of thinking through the unique implications for your ministry in your context. The last thing I want to see happen is for these ideas to become a commodity you think you must consume. This book is a commodity you have consumed, but the gifts of the Holy Spirit, which empower you to do this ministry, are not commodities.

Help Young People Develop a Critical Eye toward Advertising and Consumption

This implication is repeated from chapter 4, but it applies again here. Train your own eye to see how our young people become commodified and how they become targeted as consumers. Teach others to notice it as well. Help them notice when the church, and especially youth ministry events, start to present faith as a product for consumption or to approach young people primarily as consumers.

Learn How They Create

We do not make our young people into cocreators. They already are cocreators. Take time to learn how the young people in your congregation are already creating. They might make circuits or robots. They might make portraits or sculptures. They might write poetry, songs, or stories. They might create outfits or hair-dos. They might create friendships and networks. Organize an art show or a rotating art gallery in your congregation's building to showcase the artwork and creative expressions of your young people. Host a recital where all your young musicians can show the beautiful sound they create. Go with a group from your congregation to see your young people when they are in plays, musicals, sporting events, or debates. As you learn how they are already creating, help them see what they are doing as the work of cocreating that wholesome future with God for us all. They are not consuming experiences. They are not creating products for others to consume. They are not building résumés or college application credits. They are creating a future for God's world.

Teach Them How to Create

If the young people in your congregation do not see what they are already doing as cocreating, help them become aware. We can learn a lot from the field of education here. Service learning, experiential learning, critical pedagogy, project-based learning, problem-based learning, collaborative inquiry, STEM, STEAM, youth-led community organizing, and design thinking in education are all methods used by educators and youth workers to teach young people how to create. You will learn a lot from researching these approaches or speaking with teachers in your community who are implementing these methods. At Augsburg University's Riverside Innovation Hub, we are working to develop a method that will help faith communities engage their contexts in this type of creative process.[31] We use a method that teaches people how to walk with and accompany their neighbor, learning to hear their neighbors' stories. From there, the faith community moves into a time of interpretation, learning to weave together their neighbors' stories, their own stories, and God's story. This leads the community into a moment of discernment in which the faith community learns to listen to who God is calling them to be and what God in calling them to do in response to their neighbors' stories. Lastly, the faith community reengages with their neighbors in creative ways that proclaim hope and good news. There is no perfect way to do this work. The worst we can do is not try it at all.

Provide Opportunities to Create

Generate as many opportunities for your young people to create as possible. Once you know their gifts, their passions, and how they create, find ways for them to get to work cocreating that wholesome future. Rethink your programming and your congregation's activities to make space for your young people to create. Help them discover the issues in your congregation and in your larger community that concern them and begin working with them to design and create ways to address these concerns. Rather than planning a

> Rethink your programming and your congregation's activities to make space for your young people to create.

mission trip or service project for them, allow them to create these experiences using one of the educational methods listed in the section above. If your congregation does formal Christian education, confirmation, Bible, or catechism classes for young people, then allow them to help create the course of study based on their questions and their concerns. Not only that, allow them to teach!

Invite Your Entire Congregation to Embrace These Implications

Many congregations end up isolating their youth ministry program. Sometimes this happens intentionally, but often it is unintentional. The children and the youth spend their time at church with only those who are their same age. These same congregations most likely have several groups working to live out the mission of the congregation, such as quilters, a property committee, and an evangelism committee, to name a few. Encourage the members of these groups to invite young people into their work. Teach them how to incorporate design thinking or other engaging educational methods into their work as a group. The young people will benefit but so will the other participants. Empower your congregation to be cocreators and teach your congregation to empower young people to be cocreators. Make room for the young people on worship committees. Pastors, as part of your regular sermon preparation practices, invite a group of young people each week to sit with you and talk about the texts you will be preaching on. Become creative with how you empower cocreation.

Discussion Questions

1. How have you been a cocreator in the past? In what ways would you love to be practicing cocreation right now?

2. Look for examples of how your young people are creating in your congregation and community. Talk about these examples. How does this discussion inspire creating in your congregation?

3. In what ways might your congregation's ministry with young people still be dependent on the assumption that they are commodified consumers?

4. How would your congregation's ministry with young people change if you took them seriously as created cocreators?

5. What is one thing your congregation can do right away to begin implementing at least one of the strategies listed above?

CONCLUSION

We have taken a long, loving look at our young people in order to see how they are in bondage to the image of undeveloped consumer we force upon them. We have seen how this undeveloped consumer is a false identity and yet wields great power and influence. God's vision for our young people in the Bible and Martin Luther's theology of vocation provide a foundation for us to build a different vision of life for our young people. This vision is the *called cocreator*. The called cocreator is an old concept that connects us to the God who has made us to be cocreators from the beginning. It is new in that it has yet to fully shape our engagement with our young people.

Our young people have patiently taught us many things. They are not undeveloped. They are gifted and called by God to do their part in God's work of healing creation. They are eager to do this work. Our young people are not identity-less. They are named and claimed as children of God, adopted into God's timeless covenant community. They are eager to become who they already are. Our young people are not self-centered. They are created in God's relational image and move through life in highly relational ways. They are eager to connect with all of creation in life-giving ways. Our young people are not commodified consumers. They are created cocreators with whom God shares power in order to continue bringing life to our world. Open your eyes and you will see the creativity of our young people breathing new life into our churches and communities.

The ideas shared in this book are only as powerful as your tenacity to implement them. My goal was to open our eyes collectively to see our young people in a new light. It was not my intention to provide one more technological gadget full of promises it cannot keep. The bondage our young people experience from the undeveloped consumer is felt at the individual level. Therefore, the liberation they desire will also have to be experienced at the individual level. Quick programmatic changes will help, but the good news we all seek will come through the slow and steady tending of real relationships. Samuel did not need an event, an outing, a curriculum, a concert, or a service project to learn to hear God's voice calling him. Samuel needed Eli.

Our young people are gifts to our churches and to our world. But we often keep these gifts suppressed in the shell of the undeveloped consumer. Even the young person who is aware of her gifts will be reluctant to share them for fear of coming across as childish, insecure, selfish, or just another product. After all, this is what she has heard adult society telling her for a lifetime.

> Our young people are gifts to our churches and to our world.

CONCLUSION

On Wednesday, February 14, 2018, around 2:20 p.m. Eastern Time, nineteen-year-old Nikolas Cruz walked into Marjory Stoneman Douglas High School in Parkland, Florida, with an AR-15 assault rifle and began shooting students and teachers. He murdered seventeen people and wounded another fourteen. We have had far too many school shootings in our country over the last decade. But something different happened in the wake of the Stoneman Douglas shooting. The students began to rise up and demand stricter gun-control laws.

At an anti-gun rally in Fort Lauderdale just two days after the shooting, Marjory Stoneman Douglas senior Emma Gonzalez gave an emotional and powerful speech that went viral. In this speech, Gonzalez said, "We are going to be the kids you read about in textbooks. Not because we're going to be another statistic about mass shooting in America, but because . . . we are going to be the last mass shooting."[1]

On Tuesday, February 20, 2018—with survivors of the Stoneman Douglas shooting present—Florida's Republican House of Representatives cowardly voted 36–71, killing a measure that would have allowed the House to debate a motion banning assault rifles and high-capacity magazines. Gonzalez and fellow survivors then organized a rally against mass shootings called March for Our Lives, which took place on March 24, 2018. Anywhere from two to eight hundred thousand people came out for the main event in Washington, DC, and there were more than eight hundred other such marches across the United States and several more around the globe.[2]

Up to this point, this story serves as a living example of how our young people are living their lives as called cocreators and how some adults are treating them like undeveloped consumers. Many adults do not take these young people's fears or hopes seriously. Their own state-elected officials could not even rise to the occasion six days after the shooting, as survivors of the shooting stood in their midst. Some have accused these students of being actors.

This story continues to unfold as I work on the final edits of this book. By the time you are holding this book in your hands, we will have a better idea of how our government has listened to and responded to these young people. I include this event here in the conclusion of this book because I believe this is such a powerful example of young people finding their voice and making it heard, of embracing their God-given power and using it to refashion their world. It appears to be a watershed moment. Our young people have had enough. They are scared and angry and are tired of watching those who should be protecting them placing their loyalty elsewhere. We will see where this goes. Will the adult world take these young people seriously? Reread the poems scattered throughout this book and imagine them being written by these survivors or for them. Reread Samuel's call story in chapter 3 and imagine Emma Gonzalez in Samuel's role. Our young people are literally dying from our assumption that they are disposable and undeveloped consumers. They are rising up. They are finding their voices. They have heard their call. Will we listen?

God has created our young people for relationships, Jesus has freed them for these relationships, and the Holy Spirit is blowing our gifted young people into the world on behalf of their neighbors. Eli saw this in Samuel. Even though Eli knew it would not turn out well for himself, he mentored Samuel so that Samuel could hear God's call to become a called cocreator. If we truly long for our young people to be liberated from the bondage that threatens them, then we must be just as willing as Eli to risk everything for them. God's words of hope for our world are swelling up within our young people. They are singing in their cages. When liberated from the undeveloped consumer, their words will be loud, they will not fall to the ground, and they will make the ears of everyone who hears them tingle.

NOTES

INTRODUCTION

1. Maya Angelou, "Caged Bird," in *The Complete Poetry* (New York: Random House, 2015), 189.
2. Walter Brueggemann, "Counterscript: Living with the Elusive God," *Christian Century* 122, no. 24 (2005): 22–28.
3. Richard M. Lerner, *The Good Teen: Rescuing Adolescence from the Myths of the Storm and Stress Years* (New York: Three Rivers, 2007), 31.
4. Andrew Root, "Youth Ministry as a Magical Technology: Moving Toward the Theological," *Catalyst*, November 20, 2013, https://tinyurl.com/y9wmo8oc.
5. Philip Hefner, *The Human Factor* (Minneapolis: Fortress Press, 1993).

CHAPTER 1: THE UNDEVELOPED CONSUMER: YOUTH IN BONDAGE TO THE ADOLESCENT

1. "The key contribution of the 1900–1920 period was not the discovery of adolescence, for in one form or another a recognition of changes at puberty, even drastic changes, had been present long before 1900. Rather, it was the invention of the adolescent, the youth whose social definition—and indeed, whose whole being—was determined by a biological process of maturation." Joseph F.

Kett, *Rites of Passage: Adolescence in America 1790 to the Present* (New York: Basic, 1977), 243.

2. Douglas John Hall, "What Is Theology?" *Cross Currents* 53, no. 2 (2003): 177–79.

3. I will say more about intersectionality a little later in this chapter, but for now here is a helpful definition: "Human identities that are tied to systemic privilege and oppression can intersect with one another and thus shape the unique ways that people experience aspects of life. These identities have to do with sex, gender, sexual orientation, age, ability, race, ethnicity, nationality/citizenship, social class, economics and religion, to name a few. For example, this means that the gender-based violence and oppression experienced by a lesbian woman of color will be different than that experienced by an economically impoverished gender non-conforming white person. All human identities and all forms of privilege and oppression are made up of many intersections." ELCA Taskforce on Women and Justice, *Faith, Sexism, Justice: Conversations toward a Social Statement* (Chicago: Evangelical Lutheran Church in America, 2016), 113.

4. Nancy Lesko, *Act Your Age! A Cultural Construction of Adolescence* (New York: Routledge Falmer, 2001), 6.

5. Lesko, *Act Your Age!*, 50.

6. Erik H. Erikson, *Childhood and Society*, 2nd ed. (New York: W. W. Norton, 1963), 247–74.

7. Erikson, *Childhood and Society*, 262.

8. "Word of the Year 2013," *Oxford Dictionaries* (online), https://tinyurl.com/y7w56wpc; Stephanie Mlot, "Scrabble Dictionary Adds 'Selfie,' 'Hashtag,' Others," PCMag.com, August 5, 2014, https://tinyurl.com/ydyw6req.

9. David Elkind, "Egocentrism in Adolescence," *Child Development* 38, no. 4 (1967): 1025–34.

10. George W. Bush, "At O'Hare, President Says 'Get on Board,'" The White House Archives, September 27, 2001, https://tinyurl.com/y85ykhv5.

11. Thomas Hine, *The Rise and Fall of the American Teenager* (New York: Perennial, 2000), 234.

12. Henry A. Giroux, *Youth in a Suspect Society: Democracy or Disposability?* (New York: Palgrave Macmillan, 2010), 34.
13. Giroux, *Youth in a Suspect Society*, 54.

CHAPTER 2: VOCATION AS LIBERATION FROM THE UNDEVELOPED CONSUMER

1. Marcia J. Bunge with Terrence E. Fretheim and Beverly Roberts Gaventa, eds., *The Child in the Bible* (Grand Rapids: Eerdmans, 2008). Marcia J. Bunge, ed., *The Child in Christian Thought* (Grand Rapids: Eerdmans, 2001). I highly recommend these two excellent, comprehensive volumes edited by Marcia Bunge that cover both a biblical and theological understanding of young people. I limit my use of these volumes to two chapters that, in my opinion, provide an excellent summary of the key insights from both the Old and New Testaments.
2. Walter Brueggemann, "Vulnerable Children, Divine Passion, and Human Obligation," in Bunge, Fretheim, and Roberts Gaventa, *Child in the Bible*, 399–400.
3. Brueggemann, "Vulnerable Children," 409.
4. Stephen Prothero, *God Is Not One: The Eight Rival Religions That Run the World—And Why Their Differences Matter* (New York: HarperOne, 2010), 253.
5. Brueggemann, "Vulnerable Children," 415.
6. Judith M. Gundry-Volf, "The Least and the Greatest: Children in the New Testament," in Bunge, *Child in Christian Thought*, 32.
7. Gundry-Volf, "Least and the Greatest," 34.
8. Gundry-Volf, "Least and the Greatest," 32.
9. Gundry-Volf, "Least and the Greatest," 32.
10. Gundry-Volf, "Least and the Greatest," 37–38.
11. Bonnie J. Miller-McLemore, *Let the Children Come: Reimagining Childhood from a Christian Perspective* (San Francisco: Jossey-Bass, 2003), 84.
12. Douglas J. Schuurman, *Vocation: Discerning Our Callings in Life* (Grand Rapids: Eerdmans, 2004). Luther was not the only Protestant Reformer to rework the church's understanding of Christian vocation, but I find his nuances and use of the doctrine to be more

grounded than some of the others. This project does not allow the space to compare and contrast the other views. If interested in that conversation, I recommend reading this text by Schuurman.

13. Martin Luther, *The Freedom of a Christian*, trans. Mark D. Tranvik (Minneapolis: Fortress Press, 2008), 50.

14. *Freedom of a Christian* is the text where Luther most clearly develops his doctrine of vocation. Gustaf Wingren, *Luther on Vocation*, trans. Carl C. Rasmussen (Eugene, OR: Wipf & Stock, 2004) is the seminal work that explains Luther's understanding of vocation and its place within his larger theological system. The diagram (figure 2) and section are based on these two texts.

15. Wingren, *Luther on Vocation*, 203.

16. You can learn more about these programs at the websites for the High School Youth Theology Institutes (www.hsyti.org) and the Lilly Youth Theology Network (www.youththeology.org).

17. David F. White, *Dreamcare: A Theology of Youth, Spirit, and Vocation* (Eugene, OR: Cascade, 2013), 17–18.

18. White, *Dreamcare*, 17.

19. David F. White, *Practicing Discernment with Youth: A Transformative Youth Ministry Approach* (Cleveland: Pilgrim, 2005), 48.

20. Dori Grinenko Baker and Joyce Ann Mercer, *Lives to Offer: Accompanying Youth on Their Vocational Quests* (Cleveland: Pilgrim, 2007), 4.

21. Luther, *Freedom of a Christian*, 79–80.

22. Luther, *Freedom of a Christian*, 50.

23. Wingren, *Luther on Vocation*, 46.

24. Luther, *Freedom of a Christian*, 73. Tranvik translates Luther's description of the spirit in which one acts vocationally as the "spirit of spontaneous love."

25. Wingren, *Luther on Vocation*, 59.

26. Wingren, *Luther on Vocation*, 214.

27. Wingren, *Luther on Vocation*, 33.

28. Jeremy P. Myers, "Adolescent Experiences of Christ's Presence and Activity in the Evangelical Lutheran Church in America," *Journal of Youth and Theology* 7, no. 1 (2008): 27–43.

29. Myers, "Adolescent Experiences," 32.

NOTES

CHAPTER 3: CALLED

1. Boyd Huppert, "Land of 10,000 Stories: Students 'Just Say Yes' to Their Anti-Drug," KARE-11, updated March 15, 2017, https://tinyurl.com/yblawhcg.
2. www.strengths-explorer.com and www.strengthsquest.com.
3. Peter L. Benson, *Sparks: How Parents Can Ignite the Hidden Strengths of Teenagers* (San Francisco: Jossey-Bass, 2008). You can also learn more about Sparks at Search Institute's website, www.search-institute.org/sparks.
4. Luther K. Snow, "The Quick and Simple Congregational Asset-Mapping Experience," Alban Institute, 2004, PDF, https://tinyurl.com/y8eomxa9.

CHAPTER 4: CHILD OF GOD

1. Erik H. Erikson, *Childhood and Society*, 2nd ed. (New York: W. W. Norton, 1963), 262.
2. Carol Gilligan, *In a Different Voice: Psychological Theory and Women's Development* (Cambridge, MA: Harvard University Press, 1982), 12.
3. Paul Ramsey, *Basic Christian Ethics* (Louisville: Westminster John Knox, 1993), 250–64. This section is a summary of Ramsey's excellent synopsis of both the relational and substantialist explanations of the *imago Dei*.
4. Douglas John Hall, *Imaging God: Dominion as Stewardship* (Eugene, OR: Wipf & Stock, 2004), 98.
5. David L. Bartlett, "Adoption in the Bible," in *The Child in the Bible*, ed. Marcia J. Bunge with Terence E. Fretheim and Beverly Roberts Gaventa (Grand Rapids: Eerdmans, 2008), 395.
6. Mary Ann Hinsdale, "Infinite Openness to the Infinite: Karl Rahner's Contribution to Modern Catholic Thought on the Child," in *The Child in Christian Thought*, ed. Marcia J. Bunge (Grand Rapids: Eerdmans, 2001), 428.
7. Jane Hu, "When We Were Seventeen: A History in 47 Covers," *The Awl*, September 28, 2012, https://tinyurl.com/y7z94sto.

8. The documentary is now somewhat dated simply because it deals with popular culture. However, it is still worth watching: "The Merchants of Cool," *Frontline*, PBS, https://tinyurl.com/z3q78tx.
9. "Synopsis," *Frontline*, accessed July 30, 2017, https://tinyurl.com/yb8mb23u.
10. Elizabeth Conde-Frazier, *Listen to the Children: Conversations with Immigrant Families* (Valley Forge, PA: Judson, 2011), 67.
11. Letty M. Russell, *Church in the Round: Feminist Interpretation of the Church* (Louisville: Westminster John Knox, 1993), 161.
12. Eric D. Barreto, "Negotiating Difference: Theology and Ethnicity in the Acts of the Apostles," *Word and World* 31, no. 2 (2011): 132.
13. Barreto, "Negotiating Difference," 131.
14. Evelyn L. Parker, *Trouble Don't Last Always: Emancipatory Hope among African American Adolescents* (Cleveland: Pilgrim, 2003), 37.
15. Parker, *Trouble Don't Last Always*, 47.
16. Erin Hansert, Facebook message to author, February 26, 2017.
17. Michael Lipka, "The Most and Least Racially Diverse U.S. Religious Groups," Fact Tank, Pew Research Center, July 27, 2015, https://tinyurl.com/y8ewk5dr.
18. Russell, *Church in the Round*, 161.
19. Rozella White, discussion with the author, August 2017.
20. Rozella White, discussion with the author, August 2017.
21. Peter Menzel and Charles C Mann. *Material World: A Global Family Portrait* (San Francisco: Sierra Club Books, 1994).
22. Simba Runyowa, "Microaggressions Matter," *The Atlantic*, September 18, 2015, https://tinyurl.com/y88b3mhz. This is an excellent article that explains microaggressions, how they do damage, and why they matter.

CHAPTER 5: RELATIONAL

1. Mary Oliver, "Wild Geese," in *Dream Work* (Boston: Atlantic Monthly Press, 1986), 14.
2. Nicholas Epley, Carey K. Morewedge, and Boaz Keysar, "Perspective Taking in Children and Adults: Equivalent Egocentrism but

Differential Correction," *Journal of Experimental Social Psychology* 40, no. 6 (2004): 760–68.

3. David Elkind, "Egocentrism in Adolescence," *Child Development* 38, no. 4 (1967): 1029.

4. Elkind, "Egocentrism in Adolescence," 1029–30.

5. Terence E. Fretheim, *God and World in the Old Testament: A Relational Theology of Creation* (Nashville: Abingdon, 2005), 16.

6. Fretheim, *God and World in the Old Testament*, 17.

7. Fretheim, *God and World in the Old Testament*, 19.

8. Fretheim, *God and World in the Old Testament*, 16–17.

9. Fretheim, *God and World in the Old Testament*, 17.

10. Fretheim, *God and World in the Old Testament*, 19.

11. Andrew Root, *Revisiting Relational Youth Ministry: From a Strategy of Influence to a Theology of Incarnation* (Downers Grove, IL: InterVarsity, 2007), 100.

12. Douglas John Hall, *Imaging God: Dominion as Stewardship* (Eugene, OR: Wipf & Stock, 2004), 134.

13. "Developmental Relationships," Search Institute, 2016, https://tinyurl.com/y7ph69e9.

14. Roberto S. Goizueta, *Caminemos con Jesús: Toward a Hispanic/Latino Theology of Accompaniment* (Maryknoll, NY: Orbis, 1995), 183.

CHAPTER 6: CREATED COCREATOR

1. Dominique Christina, "The Dream about Shouting," in *The Bones, the Breaking, the Balm: A Colored Girl's Hymnal* (Brooklyn, NY: Penmanship Books, 2014), 14.

2. Marvin E. Goldberg, Gerald J. Gorn, Laura A. Peracchio, and Gary Bamossy, "Understanding Materialism among Youth," *Journal of Consumer Psychology* 13, no. 3 (2003): 278.

3. Goldberg, Gorn, Peracchio, and Bamossy, "Understanding Materialism," 285–86.

4. Deborah Roedder John, "Consumer Socialization of Children: A Retrospective Look at Twenty-Five Years of Research," *Journal of Consumer Research* 26, no. 3 (1999): 183.

5. John, "Consumer Socialization," 186–87.

6. John, "Consumer Socialization," 207.

7. Henry A. Giroux, *Youth in a Suspect Society: Democracy or Disposability?* (New York: Palgrave Macmillan, 2010), 3.

8. Benjamin R. Barber, *Consumed: How Markets Corrupt Children, Infantilize Adults, and Swallow Citizens Whole* (New York: W. W. Norton, 2007), 35.

9. Juliet B. Schor, "The Commodification of Childhood: Tales from the Advertising Front Lines," *Hedgehog Review* 5, no. 2 (2003): 9–10.

10. Tom Reichert, "The Prevalence of Sexual Imagery in Ads Targeted to Young Adults," *The Journal of Consumer Affairs* 37, no. 2 (2003): 411.

11. "Trafficking in Persons Report," US Department of State, June 2017, p. 34, https://tinyurl.com/y7fkzou5.

12. Giroux, *Youth in a Suspect Society*, 49–62.

13. Giroux, *Youth in a Suspect Society*, 54.

14. Roberto S. Goizueta, *Caminemos con Jesús: Toward a Hispanic/ Latino Theology of Accompaniment* (Maryknoll, NY: Orbis, 1995), 189–90.

15. Philip Hefner, *The Human Factor* (Minneapolis: Fortress Press, 1993), 39. Some have critiqued Hefner's formula for giving the human being too much power and potentially equating the created with the Creator. Hefner has considered these critiques yet sees his formula as the most constructive and faithful way forward. Hefner says, "I have been urged by critics to substitute another term, such as creative creatures, for created co-creator. However, I find neither this term nor other proposed alternatives to be adequate for conceptualizing the dual nature of the human being—a creature who has been brought into existence by nature's processes, and who has been given by that nature the role of free co-creator within those same processes."

16. Hefner, *Human Factor*, 27.

17. Evelyn L. Parker, ed., *The Sacred Selves of Adolescent Girls: Hard Stories of Race, Class, and Gender* (Cleveland: Pilgrim, 2006), 163–64.

18. Philip J. Hefner, "The Evolution of the Created Co-Creator," *Currents in Theology and Mission* 15, no. 6 (1988): 522.
19. Philip J. Hefner, "Can the Created Co-Creator Be Lutheran? A Response to Svend Andersen," *Dialog* 44, no. 2 (2005): 187.
20. Gregory R. Peterson, "The Created Co-Creator: What It Is and Is Not," *Zygon* 39, no. 4 (2004): 829.
21. Peterson, "Created Co-Creator," 829.
22. Daniel Erlander, *Manna and Mercy: A Brief History of God's Unfolding Promise to Mend the Entire Universe* (Mercer Island, WA: Order of Saints Martin and Teresa, 1992), 7–9.
23. Philip Hefner, "The Human Being," in *Christian Dogmatics*, ed. Carl E. Braaten, Robert W. Jenson, and Gerhard O. Forde, 2 vols. (Philadelphia: Fortress Press, 1984), 1:328.
24. Hercules T. Rockefeller, "South Minneapolis Kids Respond to Animal Cruelty with Community Solidarity," Twin Cities Daily Planet, August 17, 2012, https://tinyurl.com/y9juwa8b.
25. Rockefeller, "South Minneapolis Kids."
26. Hefner, *Human Factor*, 27.
27. Peter L. Benson, *Sparks: How Parents Can Ignite the Hidden Strengths of Teenagers* (San Francisco: Jossey-Bass, 2008).
28. "The Hickory Playground," Facebook, https://tinyurl.com/yadc7j2o.
29. "The Hickory Playground," Facebook, https://tinyurl.com/yadc7j2o.
30. Hefner, *Human Factor*, 27.
31. "Riverside Innovation Hub," Augsburg University, www.augsburg.edu/riversidehub.

CONCLUSION

1. "Florida Student Emma Gonzalez to Lawmakers and Gun Advocates: 'We Call BS,'" CNN, February 17, 2018, https://tinyurl.com/y7q3n37z.
2. "How Many People Attended March for Our Lives? Crowd in D.C. Estimated at 200,000" CBS News, March 25, 2018, https://tinyurl.com/ya3334bl.

BIBLIOGRAPHY

Angelou, Maya. *The Complete Poetry*. New York: Random House, 2015.

Baker, Dori Grinenko, and Joyce Ann Mercer. *Lives to Offer: Accompanying Youth on Their Vocational Quests*. Cleveland: Pilgrim, 2007.

Barber, Benjamin R. *Consumed: How Markets Corrupt Children, Infantilize Adults, and Swallow Citizens Whole*. New York: W. W. Norton, 2007.

Barreto, Eric D. "Negotiating Difference: Theology and Ethnicity in the Acts of the Apostles." *Word and World* 31, no. 2 (2011): 129–37.

Bartlett, David L. "Adoption in the Bible." In *The Child in the Bible*, edited by Marcia J. Bunge with Terence E. Fretheim and Beverly Roberts Gaventa, 375–98. Grand Rapids: Eerdmans, 2008.

Benson, Peter L. *Sparks: How Parents Can Ignite the Hidden Strengths of Teenagers*. San Francisco: Jossey-Bass, 2008.

Brueggemann, Walter. "Counterscript: Living with the Elusive God." *Christian Century* 122, no. 24 (2005): 22–28.

———. "Vulnerable Children, Divine Passion, and Human Obligation." In *The Child in the Bible*, edited by Marcia J. Bunge, with Terrence E. Fretheim and Beverly Roberts, 399–422. Grand Rapids: Eerdmans, 2008.

Bunge, Marcia J., ed. *The Child in Christian Thought.* Grand Rapids: Eerdmans, 2001.

Bunge, Marcia J., with Terrence E. Fretheim and Beverly Roberts, eds. *The Child in the Bible.* Grand Rapids: Eerdmans, 2008.

Bush, George W. "At O'Hare, President Says 'Get on Board.'" The White House Archives, September 27, 2001. https://tinyurl.com/y85ykhv5.

CBS News. "How Many People Attended March for Our Lives? Crowd in D.C. Estimated at 200,000." March 25, 2018. https://tinyurl.com/ya3334bl.

Christina, Dominique. *The Bones, the Breaking, the Balm: A Colored Girl's Hymnal.* Brooklyn, NY: Penmanship Books, 2014.

CNN. "Florida Student Emma Gonzalez to Lawmakers and Gun Advocates: 'We Call BS.'" February 17, 2018. https://tinyurl.com/y7q3n37z.

Conde-Frazier, Elizabeth. *Listen to the Children: Conversations with Immigrant Families.* Valley Forge, PA: Judson, 2011.

ELCA Taskforce on Women and Justice. *Faith, Sexism, Justice: Conversations toward a Social Statement.* Chicago: Evangelical Lutheran Church in America, 2016.

Elkind, David. "Egocentrism in Adolescence." *Child Development* 38, no. 4 (1967): 1025–34.

Epley, Nicholas, Carey K. Morewedge, and Boaz Keysar. "Perspective Taking in Children and Adults: Equivalent

Egocentrism but Differential Correction." *Journal of Experimental Social Psychology* 40, no. 6 (2004): 760–68.

Erickson, Erik H. *Childhood and Society*. 2nd ed. New York: W. W. Norton, 1963.

Erlander, Daniel. *Manna and Mercy: A Brief History of God's Unfolding Promise to Mend the Entire Universe*. Mercer Island, WA: Order of Saints Martin and Teresa, 1992.

Fretheim, Terence E. *God and World in the Old Testament: A Relational Theology of Creation*. Nashville: Abingdon, 2005.

Gilligan, Carol. *In a Different Voice: Psychological Theory and Women's Development*. Cambridge, MA: Harvard University Press, 1982.

Giroux, Henry A. *Youth in a Suspect Society: Democracy or Disposability?* New York: Palgrave Macmillan, 2010.

Goizueta, Roberto S. *Caminemos con Jesús: Toward a Hispanic/Latino Theology of Accompaniment*. Maryknoll, NY: Orbis, 1995.

Goldberg, Marvin E., Gerald J. Gorn, Laura A. Peracchio, and Gary Bamossy. "Understanding Materialism among Youth." *Journal of Consumer Psychology* 13, no. 3 (2003): 278–88.

Gundry-Volf, Judith M. "The Least and the Greatest: Children in the New Testament." In *The Child in Christian Thought*, edited by Marcia J. Bunge, 29–60. Grand Rapids: Eerdmans, 2001.

Hall, John Douglas. *Imaging God: Dominion as Stewardship*. Eugene, OR: Wipf & Stock, 2004.

Hefner, Philip J. "Can the Created Co-Creator Be Lutheran? A Response to Svend Andersen." *Dialog* 44, no. 2 (2005): 184–88.

———. "The Evolution of the Created Co-Creator." *Currents in Theology and Mission* 15, no. 6 (1988): 512–25

———. "The Human Being." In *Christian Dogmatics*, edited by Carl E. Braaten, Robert W. Jenson, and Gerhard O. Forde, vol. 1, 323–40. Philadelphia: Fortress Press, 1984.

———. *The Human Factor*. Minneapolis: Augsburg Fortress, 1993.

Hine, Thomas. *The Rise and Fall of the American Teenager*. New York: Perennial, 2000.

Hinsdale, Mary Ann. "Infinite Openness to the Infinite: Karl Rahner's Contribution to Modern Catholic Thought on the Child." In *The Child in Christian Thought*, edited by Marcia J. Bunge, 406–45. Grand Rapids: Eerdmans, 2001.

Hu, Jane. "When We Were Seventeen: A History in 47 Covers." *The Awl*, September 28, 2012. https://tinyurl.com/y7z94sto.

Huppert, Boyd. "Land of 10,000 Stories: Students 'Just Say Yes' to Their Anti-Drug." KARE-11, updated March 15, 2017. https://tinyurl.com/yblawhcg.

John, Deborah Roedder. "Consumer Socialization of Children: A Retrospective Look at Twenty-Five Years of Research." *Journal of Consumer Research* 26, no. 3 (1999): 183–213.

Kett, Joseph F. *Rites of Passage: Adolescence in America 1790 to the Present*. New York: Basic, 1977.

Lerner, Richard M. *The Good Teen: Rescuing Adolescence from the Myths of the Storm and Stress Years*. New York: Three Rivers, 2007.

Lesko, Nancy. *Act Your Age! A Cultural Construction of Adolescence*. New York: Routledge Falmer, 2001.

Lipka, Michael. "The Most and Least Racially Diverse U.S. Religious Groups." Fact Tank, Pew Research Center, July 27, 2015. https://tinyurl.com/y8ewk5dr.

Luther, Martin. *The Freedom of a Christian*. Translated by Mark D. Tranvik. Minneapolis: Fortress Press, 2008.

Miller-McLemore, Bonnie J. *Let the Children Come: Reimagining Childhood from a Christian Perspective*. San Francisco: Jossey-Bass, 2003.

Myers, Jeremy P. "Adolescent Experiences of Christ's Presence and Activity in the Evangelical Lutheran Church in America." *Journal of Youth and Theology* 7, no. 1 (2008): 27–43.

Oliver, Mary. *Dream Work*. Boston: Atlantic Monthly Press, 1986.

Parker, Evelyn L. *The Sacred Selves of Adolescent Girls: Hard Stories of Race, Class, and Gender*. Cleveland: Pilgrim, 2006.

———. *Trouble Don't Last Always: Emancipatory Hope among African American Adolescents*. Cleveland: Pilgrim, 2003.

Peterson, Gregory R. "The Created Co-Creator: What It Is and Is Not." *Zygon* 39, no. 4 (2004): 827–40.

Prothero, Stephen. *God Is Not One: The Eight Rival Religions That Run the World—And Why Their Differences Matter*. New York: HarperOne, 2010.

Ramsey, Paul. *Basic Christian Ethics*. Louisville: Westminster John Knox, 1993.

Reichert, Tom. "The Prevalence of Sexual Imagery in Ads Targeted to Young Adults." *The Journal of Consumer Affairs* 37, no. 2 (2003): 403–12.

Rockefeller, Hercules. "South Minneapolis Kids Respond to Animal Cruelty with Community Solidarity." Twin Cities Daily Planet, August 17, 2012. https://tinyurl.com/y9juwa8b.

Root, Andrew. *Revisiting Relational Youth Ministry: From a Strategy of Influence to a Theology of Incarnation.* Downers Grove, IL: InterVarsity, 2007.

Runyowa, Simba. "Microaggressions Matter." *The Atlantic*, September 18, 2015. https://tinyurl.com/y88b3mhz.

Russell, Letty M. *Church in the Round: Feminist Interpretation of the Church.* Louisville: Westminster John Knox, 1993.

Schor, Juliet B. "The Commodification of Childhood: Tales from the Advertising Front Lines." *Hedgehog Review* 5, no. 2 (2003): 7–23.

Schuurman, Douglas J. *Vocation: Discerning Our Callings in Life.* Grand Rapids: Eerdmans, 2004.

Snow, Luther K. "The Quick and Simple Congregational Asset-Mapping Experience." Alban Institute, 2004. PDF. https://tinyurl.com/y8eomxa9.

White, David F. *Dreamcare: A Theology of Youth, Spirit, and Vocation.* Eugene, OR: Cascade, 2013.

———. *Practicing Discernment with Youth: A Transformative Youth Ministry Approach.* Cleveland: Pilgrim, 2005.

Wingren, Gustaf. *Luther on Vocation.* Translated by Carl C. Rasmussen. Eugene, OR: Wipf & Stock, 2004.

ACKNOWLEDGMENTS

I have many people to thank for their partnership in this project. Most importantly, I want to thank the young people I have worked with at St. Philip's Lutheran Church in Fridley, Minnesota; Christ Lutheran Church in Valparaiso, Indiana; and those who have attended the Augsburg Youth Theology Institute during my tenure with the program. You are the ones who have taught me the lessons I write about in this book. You are the ones I have watched reject the label of *undeveloped consumer* and take on the mantel of *called cocreator*. I also thank the students I have had in the Youth and Family Ministry degree program at Augsburg University over the years. You have been my guinea pigs and audience as I have experimented with, taught, and honed the ideas in this book.

I am grateful to many friends who have read drafts of this book, lending their expertise in very helpful ways, including Mary Lowe, Mindy Makant, Tom Schwolert, Justin Daleiden, Hans Jorgensen, and Mark Jackson. I am appreciative of your honest critique and affirmation of this project. I would also like to thank my colleagues in the religion department at Augsburg

University. Over the last twelve years, you have taught me how to be my own brand of scholar and teacher. Your patience with me and your support of my discipline have been a true gift to me. Lastly, I am forever grateful to my family—Tracie, Elijah, Naamah, and Mom—you have sacrificed a lot to give me the time to write this book over the past year. Thank you for your love and support. I know the things in this book are true because these people have shown me they are true.

THEOLOGY FOR CHRISTIAN MINISTRY

Informing and inspiring Christian leaders and communities to proclaim God's *Word* to a *World* God created and loves. Articulating the fullness of both realities and the creative intersection between them.

Word & World Books is a partnership between Luther Seminary, the board of the periodical *Word & World*, and Fortress Press.

Books in the series include:

Future Faith: Ten Challenges Reshaping Christianity in the 21st Century by Wesley Granberg-Michaelson (2018)

Liberating Youth from Adolescence by Jeremy Paul Myers (2018)

Elders Rising: The Promise and Peril of Aging by Roland D. Martinson (2018)